orchids

orchids

A Splendid Obsession

Wilma and Brian Rittershausen

Endorsed by the Royal Horticultural Society

Photography by Linda Burgess

SOMA

Page one: *Miltoniopsis* Eureka
Page two: *Phragmipedium* Sedenii
Left: *Brassia verrucosa*
Opposite: *Encyclia cochleata*

First published 1999 in Great Britain by
Quadrille Publishing Limited.
North American edition published 1999 by
Soma Books, by arrangement with Quadrille.

Soma Books is an imprint of Bay Books & Tapes,
555 De Haro St., No. 220, San Francisco, CA 94107.

For the Quadrille edition:
Editorial Director: Jane O' Shea
Art Director: Mary Evans
Project Editor: Carole McGlynn
Design: Paul Welti
Editorial Assistant: Caroline Perkins
Special Photography: Linda Burgess
Production: Vincent Smith

For the-Soma edition:
North American Editor: Andrea Chesman

Library of Congress Cataloging-in-Publication Data
on file with the Publisher

ISBN   1-57959-054-3

Printed in Hong Kong
10 9 8 7 6 5 4 3 2 1
Distributed by Publishers Group West

contents

introduction

Orchids have captivated the imagination for hundreds of years. Mysterious and alluring, they are fascinating plants of infinite beauty and extreme variety. The aim of this book is to introduce readers to their extraordinary diversity and to unravel a little of their mystery. We have deliberately selected orchids that are both simple to care for and readily available, to give a tantalizing glimpse into the world's most beautiful flowers. The majority of those chosen are easy to grow in the home or the greenhouse without any previous skill or special equipment, so they are ideal for the amateur, even the beginner, to enjoy. Since many have been bred and raised by the world's best hybridizers especially for the home orchid grower, they may well provide the starting point for what could become a lifelong interest. Dedicated orchid growers will also find much to interest them among new hybrids not seen before. The exquisite blooms of all these orchids will give years of pleasure in return for the minimum of attention.

Part I of the book, Origins of Orchids, takes a brief look at the romantic history of orchid discovery, as well as providing an insight into their fascinating life cycle, with photographs of the main types illustrating differences in their structure. Part II, A Collection of Orchids, is the heart of the book, in which we take a close look at the flowers of individual species and hybrids. Divided into three chapters according to temperature needs, each entry has a detailed description of the orchid, with a brief story of its origins and breeding. Tabular information at the end gives at-a-glance details of size (flower, plant, and flower spike where applicable); this will help you decide which plants you have room for. Details of watering requirements, ideal position, and temperature range are given only where they differ from those in the genus introduction, where more cultivation information will also be found; recommended pot sizes are for an adult plant. In Part III, the practicalities of growing orchids, from potting to propagation, are clearly explained and illustrated.

At Burnham Nurseries, we have been involved with the growing of quality orchids for 50 years. During this time, we have witnessed a greatly increased and enriched variety of modern hybrids from all around the world coming into cultivation here. Most of the orchids in the book can be seen in their season at the nursery, showing that, wherever they come from, they will thrive and produce their wonderful blooms anywhere, given the right care and conditions.

Wilma and Brian Rittershausen

An indication of the huge diversity of shape and color to be found among orchids is seen here in the species *Epidendrum pseudopidendrum* (above left) and *Aspasia lunata* (right).

s u p r e

Orchids hold many secrets. Their origins are steeped in mystery and the mists of time, and no one can be sure when orchids first appeared on earth. Because of their relatively soft vegetative parts and the tropical conditions prevailing as they evolved, very little fossil evidence has been discovered. This has given scientists scant evidence to work from and without these geological records into the past much of the orchid's prehistory is lost to us and all theories are therefore speculative. Examples of prehistoric bees have been found in amber and it is their modern descendants that retain close relationships with orchids, which may provide some proof of their great age.

macy

of orchids

The evolution of orchids

Orchids are thought to have originated during the early Cretaceous period, some 120 million years ago, when the continents we know today were breaking away from the original great land mass of Pangaea. At this time the first orchids already existed, possibly occupying an area that is now Malaysia. As the tectonic plates of this supercontinent slowly drifted apart, so the orchids moved with them and became dispersed around the world.

One of the orchids that was once widespread across this ancient land mass was *Vanilla*, whose pods are used for flavoring. The original position of this genus on Pangaea can be related directly to where vanillas are found growing naturally today. From their central location, they were carried across the oceans toward their present homes in Africa, South America to the west, and Malaysia to the east. *Dendrobium* is another huge orchid genus that also has an extensive range and that diversified into one of the largest genera, containing nearly 1,000 species found throughout China, India, Southeast Asia, Malaysia, Australia, and New Zealand. A further genus of great travelers, the slipper orchids (*Cypripedium*), circled the globe to straddle North America, extending into Europe, to Russia, China, and Japan, but not appearing anywhere south of the equator. The related *Paphiopedilum* slipper orchids spread down from China and India to Southeast Asia, including Indonesia, while their relatives, *Phragmipedium*, continued in a similar march through Central America to beyond the Isthmus of Panama, into the Andes of South America.

While the most adaptable orchids have expanded over a huge area, others that are much more specialized have hardly moved at all, and their habitat is more localized. This is true of *Cattleya*, found only in South and Central America, which may indicate that these and related genera are younger than the more primitive vanillas, or that they were insufficiently widespread to be carried on more than one piece of the disintegrating supercontinent.

Ten thousand years ago, the last Ice Age covered much of the northern hemisphere, but as the ice receded and the frozen earth warmed up, abundant life returned to colonize the land again. In evolutionary terms, this period is very short, so the flora in this part of the globe is limited both in numbers and in diversity of species. Britain, for example, is home to only about fifty-five native orchid species compared to the tens of thousands that arise in the world's tropical rain forests, which were not affected by the Ice Age to the same extent, and where evolution continued unhindered for hundreds of thousands of years.

Vanilla planifolia (left) is a primitive orchid first cultivated for its vanilla flavoring by the Aztecs of Mexico.

Dendrobium infundibulum (right) is a showy species from the Indian continent, from where it was introduced in 1864. Plentiful in Victorian England, it is today becoming rarer.

DENDROBIUM INFUNDIBULUM

Today, orchids colonize every part of the world except the arctic regions, where conditions are too severe. Everywhere else they have adapted and continued to evolve into the huge, multiformed, and highly successful family of plants called Orchidaceae. They represent the largest plant family with the greatest diversity of flora on earth. Estimates suggest the number of naturally occurring species is over 25,000, with new species being discovered even today. The species are divided into approximately 750 separate genera, according to their main characteristics. The most diverse accommodate hundreds of different species (for example, *Bulbophyllum* and *Dendrobium*), while others contain from a few (such as *Ada* and *Brassavola*) to a single specimen (*Amesiella philippinensis*).

The structure of terrestrial orchids

Orchids may be either terrestrial or epiphytic in their growth. The terrestrial orchids grow in the ground, mostly in forest or woodland leaf litter and in grassland over a wide area, but they also occur in almost any terrain, from deserts (*Eulophia petersii*) to semi-aquatic (*Hammarbya palugosa*). In arctic Russia, species of *Cypripedium* flourish under the snow, their flowers appearing as the snow recedes in spring. Even more extraordinary are the two Australian species of *Rhizanthella*, only discovered in 1928 by a farmer plowing his fields. This orchid is completely subterranean, growing and flowering entirely under the ground.

Terrestrial orchids appear in great numbers in tropical and temperate regions, where they cover hillsides in huge swathes. These plants are threatened by the advance of agriculture, the use of herbicides, and other man-related activities, such as mining and logging. Up until now they have been rarely cultivated, due to legislation protecting their environment where it still exists,

The dramatic-looking slipper orchid, *Phragmipedium longifolium* (left), is usually terrestrial, growing in the leaf litter of forests from Costa Rica to Colombia.

The exquisite flowers of *Cattleya whitei* (above) are just one manifestation of the extraordinary diversity to be found among epiphytic orchids.

as well as to the difficulty of raising them from seed and keeping them in good condition. Some of these problems recently have been overcome, however, and enthusiasts are finding that terrestrial species now can be cultivated with a measure of success.

Terrestrial orchids produce underground tubers—usually two, sometimes one—or tuberous roots from which arise an erect stem, leafed at the base and terminating in the inflorescence. The leaves vary from long and narrow to broad and short, and from one to many. Like all orchids, terrestrials are perennial herbs: They have a growing season followed by a dormant period. Once the annual growth dies down for the winter, only the flowering stem with seed capsules remains visible. Wild populations can fluctuate greatly from year to year. Where hundreds or thousands of flowering plants may be observed in one season, the following year their numbers may be only a fraction of this number.

The structure of epiphytic orchids

Epiphytic orchids grow on the trunks, branches, and extremities of trees. They are not parasitic but have adopted trees as their home in order to secure a space closer to the light and fresh air in areas where competition from other ground-dwelling plants would be intense. In this way, they have evolved an existence whereby only the toughest of plants can survive. They absorb moisture from the air through their aerial roots, without harming the tree upon which their life depends. The tree is only in danger from the largest of these epiphytes (*Grammatophyllum speciosum*), which grow on the huge ironwood trees in the Philippines. Reaching up to 5 meters (16 feet) long and completely encircling the trunk, their weight can in time bring down the tree, though the orchid will continue to grow on the ground for many more years while the tree decays. The life expectancy of most orchids is directly related to the tree's lifespan, which could be hundreds of years. Some epiphytes (*Stanhopea*, for example) produce their flowers on pendent spikes suspended below the branch upon which they grow. Here, should the tree fall, the plants will continue to grow but are unable to produce their flowers; the flowering spikes bury themselves in the leaf litter and die. During its lifetime, the orchid plant progresses forward along the branch as an advancing chain of new growths leave behind the older, dead, and decayed pseudobulbs (see page 15).

Epiphytic orchids are more diverse than the terrestrials in their plant structure, but more particularly in their flowers. With few exceptions, orchids are pollinated by insects and their methods of attracting the right one from

Coelogyne (left)
The plumped, leafed pseudobulbs of this sympodial orchid contain food reserves for the plant. New growths start from the base of the previous one. Roots also develop from the latest pseudobulb, but both leaves and roots will be outlived by the pseudobulbs, which can remain for several years after these have died. Old leafless pseudobulbs, termed back bulbs, can be used for propagation.

Cattleya (left & below)
The tall, thin pseudobulbs of this **Cattleya** hybrid each support a single semirigid leaf, identifying it as one of the unifoliate group. Cattleyas have an apical flowering habit, with long or short flower spikes produced from the top of the latest pseudobulb in season.

among these masses are fascinating and complex. With millions to choose from, each orchid has gone to extraordinary lengths to ensure that, usually, just one specific insect will be attracted to its flowers. This is why they have become so highly specialized, with huge variations between the species. While the more popular and widely cultivated orchids are easily recognized and the flower parts apparent, for every well-known type there are hundreds of lesser-known orchids, whose flower parts almost defy description, stretching the imagination and testing our powers of identification to the limit.

Found mainly in tropical regions, epiphytic orchids grow wherever it is sufficiently warm for their aerial way of life without the danger of their exposed roots becoming frozen. Their extreme southern location is in the temperate rainforests of Australia and New Zealand. Their main habitats, and the regions where they have attained their evolutionary zenith, are the equatorial forests. Here, the most flamboyant forms appear to know no bounds, their exotic beauty being unequaled in the orchid kingdom. It was these tropical epiphytic orchids that first inspired the early growers and set the horticultural world alight. But epiphytic species are in danger of extinction

Cymbidium (above)
Cymbidiums produce the most
leaves of all the popular orchid
types. Their hard pseudobulbs
are round and sheathed with
the bases of the leaves, which
are long and narrow,
gracefully arching along their
length. The flower spike is
produced from the base of the
leading pseudobulb. Extremely
free-flowering, cymbidiums can
produce up to six flower spikes
on an adult plant in a year.

too, some seriously, owing to the destruction of the tropical rain forests. This is a further threat to orchids, whose populations were gravely depleted during the nineteenth century through overcollecting. In many cases, the survival of these plants rests with botanical gardens, national parks, and nature reserves, where different orchids can be bred to establish healthy cultivated populations all around the world.

Epiphytic orchids make one of two types of growth, sympodial or monopodial. The majority of them are sympodial, producing new growth from a node at the base of the mature pseudobulb; this develops and flowers usually within one season. The plant progresses forward in this way until, over several years, a string of interdependent growths is built up, each attached to the previous one by a rhizome. Further progress is achieved when two growths are produced from one, the plant spreading out in the manner of an iris, eventually doubling its size. But orchids have no permanent structures. The roots and leaves may live for one season only, as is the case with pleiones or calanthes, or for several years, as in both the cymbidiums and the odontoglossums.

Most sympodial orchids produce pseudobulbs, which are not true bulbs, but swollen stems used for water storage. They are the longest surviving part of the plant and usually remain for five or six years. Inside they resemble a tuber rather than the embryo leaf bracts of a true bulb, such as a daffodil. These pseudobulbs vary greatly in their size and shape; they may be round, conical, or elongated into long stems or canes, depending on the genus. During their lifetime they support the orchid's leaves and roots until the leaves are shed or the roots die naturally. Once a pseudobulb becomes leafless, it is known as a back bulb and, while no longer actively supporting its own leaves and roots, it assumes a supporting role for the plant, maintaining the younger pseudobulbs with the last of its reserves. Eventually, these old pseudobulbs die, by which time several newer ones will have taken their place, perpetuating the orchid, which remains strong and continues to grow and to flower.

Odontocidium (left)
All odontoglossums are distinguished by their green, cone-shaped pseudobulbs, which typically support a pair of basal leaves and a pair of long, narrow apical leaves. The flower spikes, which appear from inside the lower leaf at its base, may be long or short, and produce few to many flowers.

Dendrobium (below)
Sympodial orchids, dendrobiums get confused with monopodial types because of their tall, cane-like pseudobulbs, which carry leaves along their entire length. New canes are produced from the base of older ones until a sizable plant is built up. While the newer canes will bloom in their season, older canes eventually become leafless and can be propagated.

Each pseudobulb may support from one to a dozen or more leaves, depending on the genus. The leaves of sympodial orchids are as varied as the pseudobulbs and may be long and narrow or short and thickened. Cattleyas produce a single broad, leathery leaf above elongated pseudobulbs, while odontoglossums and miltoniopsis produce one or two apex leaves from the top of the pseudobulbs, with two shorter basal leaves. Cymbidiums have long, narrow leaves, up to ten of them emerging from broad sheaths that enclose the pseudobulb. Some dendrobiums have very tall, canelike pseudobulbs with short, rounded leaves along their length. Other sympodial orchids, including paphiopedilums and related genera, have no pseudobulbs but instead produce sturdy growths, each with several leaves, which may be short and rounded, or long and narrow, with many examples in between. The roots of sympodial orchids may be either thin and fibrous or thick and fleshy. Plants in pots form dense rootballs that, when unwound, can reach up to a meter (3 feet) long.

Stanhopea (left)
Orchids are full of surprises. The sympodial stanhopeas produce oval, ribbed pseudobulbs, each with a single broad leaf, but the flower spikes appear from the base of the pseudobulbs and grow downward. Their tip burrows through the potting mixture to emerge beneath the plant, where the blooms open. For this reason they are grown in open slatted baskets or aquatic plastic pots.

Paphiopedilum (right)
Slipper orchids are sympodial orchids that do not produce pseudobulbs. Their several-leafed growths are produced one in front of the other in succession over the years. As the older growths die away, newer ones take on the main supportive role. Each new growth blooms once as it matures, when the flower spike emerges from between the central fleshy leaves.

Monopodial orchids exhibit a different type of growth. In these plants, which include *Vanda*, *Phalaenopsis*, and many other less well-known orchids, a single upward-growing rhizome produces leaves from the apex in alternate succession, until a fan of leaves is built up. *Phalaenopsis* are short and stout, developing one new leaf at a time, at a rate of one or two a year. The older leaves at the base are shed naturally from time to time so that the plant maintains an average of four to five leaves at any stage. Some vandas, on the other hand, continue to extend vertically, adding pairs of alternate leaves until they are up to a meter (3 feet) or more tall. As the older leaves drop away, a bare stem is left from where new aerial roots will grow. These roots, produced above the rim of the container, are thick and brittle, and can become very long.

Phalaenopsis (left)
In the monopodial growth of *Phalaenopsis*, the thick, fleshy leaves grow from a single rhizome, which extends upward as new leaves are made at the apex. Older leaves are shed naturally at about the rate new ones are made, so an adult plant rarely consists of more than five leaves. Flower spikes appear from the stem between the leaves.

Vanda (below)
The monopodial vandas produce their semirigid leaves in pairs from an ever-extending stem or rhizome. Their thick aerial roots, produced from the base and higher up the stem, are fleshy and easily snapped. Grown in open baskets, vandas have little need of potting mix, provided they are grown in a humid atmosphere where the roots can absorb moisture. Flower spikes appear between the leaves once or twice a year.

The flower structure

Orchid flowers are produced on various types of inflorescence, loosely termed "spikes," although more correctly the flowers are held on racemes. These may be basal (produced from the base of the plant, as in *Cymbidium*, *Odontoglossum*, and *Lycastes*), apical (where the spike comes from the apex of the pseudobulb, as in *Cattleya*), or axillary (as in *Vanda* and *Phalaenopsis*, where the spikes come from the stem opposite the base of the leaf). Some orchids carry a single bloom while others can support as many as a hundred or so. The most popular orchids in cultivation typically have from six to a dozen flowers on a spike that may be naturally arching, upright, or pendent or can be trained accordingly. The flowers may either appear on side branches or be produced directly from the main stem.

Orchid flowers show the widest diversity of any plant family, and this is where they differ most obviously from all other flora. With so many differences, one is led to wonder how they can all be orchids. It is their complex structure and seemingly limitless adaptations that have given rise to this infinite variation on a single theme. All orchid flowers, whether colossal or minute, whether native terrestrials or tropical epiphytes, conform to one basic pattern. Each flower consists of an outer whorl and an inner whorl. The outer whorl contains three sepals that resemble the petals in substance and color and contribute to the size and overall design of the flower. The inner whorl consists of two lateral petals, with a third petal between them, which is greatly modified to form the lip, or labellum.

The lip's function is to act like a flag, signaling to a passing pollinator. An orchid's lip makes an ideal landing platform for the visiting insect, attracted by its colored markings, distinct from the rest of the flower, and known as the honey guide. Orchid flowers take elaborate steps to ensure that the insect they wish to attract alights in exactly the right spot to accomplish pollination. Indeed, it is the specific pollinator that defines the size and shape of the lip. Where this has become diminutive, the flower may attract a certain midge or small fly. Where the lip has become almost inconspicuous it is compensated for by the enlargement or fusion of the sepals or petals. Some masdevallias produce exaggerated and highly colored sepals, while the petals are reduced to the size of the lip, hardly visible at the center of the flower.

The lips of various orchids show great ingenuity, and while some are highly complex structures, others are relatively simple in their design, but all achieve the same aim. Some are rigidly fixed, as in odontoglossums, and others have a movable hinge, found in cymbidiums, where the bee has to be of

Structure of the orchid flower

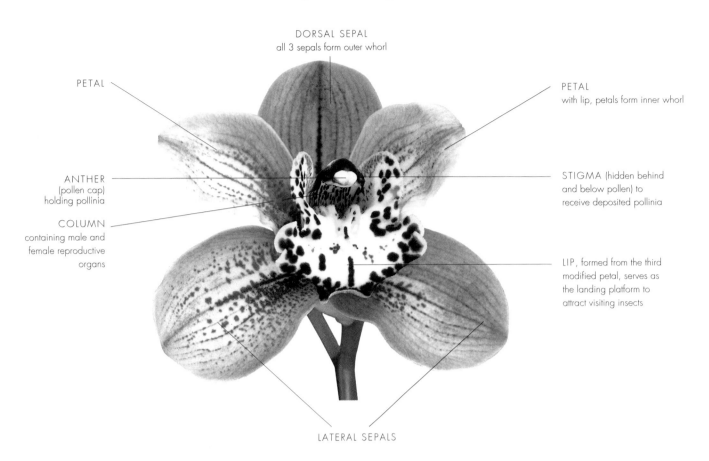

DORSAL SEPAL
all 3 sepals form outer whorl

PETAL

PETAL
with lip, petals form inner whorl

ANTHER
(pollen cap)
holding pollinia

STIGMA (hidden behind
and below pollen) to
receive deposited pollinia

COLUMN
containing male and
female reproductive
organs

LIP, formed from the third
modified petal, serves as
the landing platform to
attract visiting insects

LATERAL SEPALS

the right size to push its way into the flower. The lip of many anguloas is constructed so that it will rock back and forth at the slightest movement. Lip sizes also vary in relation to the size of the flower and reach their maximum in cattleyas and sobralias, where they become very flamboyant and the most attractive part of the flower. In oncidiums also the lip is greatly exaggerated, while the petals and sepals are reduced and partially hidden by the lip. In *Vanda (Eulanthe) sanderiana* and its hybrids, it is the large, broad sepals that are most highly patterned, while the lip is much reduced. In some species of *Bulbophyllum* and *Pleurothallis*, the lip has become almost nonexistent and a strong odor replaces it as the main attracting agent. Some lips can be hairy or have hairy adornments, such as that of *Bulbophyllum barbigerum*, which resembles a carefully constructed fishing fly and moves erratically at the slightest movement.

In the genus *Coryanthes*, the lip has become even more strangely adapted— it hangs, bucket-shaped, beneath the flower. Upon opening, the flower exudes a liquid that drips into the lip cavity, and when the flower is visited by small bees, they become extremely agitated, nibbling at the rim of the lip. Some fall or are pushed in, where they swim to a single opening, which allows them to escape, with pollinia (pollen masses) attached, to the next flower. Pollinating insects are enticed, trapped, and occasionally rewarded by the orchid they visit, but they are never intentionally killed, and no orchids ingest insects.

Paphiopedilums and related orchids are commonly called slipper orchids because their lip is modified into a pouch, which bees are encouraged to enter. Orchids are not carnivorous and the insect is always released, through a specific exit, after unintentionally delivering and collecting pollen.

In the majority of orchids, the lip is positioned at the bottom of the flower, but in a few species, like *Encyclia cochleata* and *E. radiata*, the lip is uppermost. In the bud stage of most orchids, the lip is above, but as the flower opens, the stem twists through 180 degrees until the lip is in what we think of as its normal position. Called resupination, this occurs in all popular genera.

At the center of the orchid flower is a single, fingerlike structure called the column, which contains both male and female reproductive organs. At the end of the column is the anther, or pollen cap, and beneath this easily dislodged cover, you will find the pollen. Unlike other plants, whose pollen is loose grains, the orchid pollen is held in tightly compacted masses. There are usually two, but sometimes more, little packets called pollinia; golden yellow, they are attached to a sticky disk by two threads. Having solid pollen ensures that none is wasted, unlike wind-blown pollen, which requires vast quantities to be produced because so much is lost to the air. Behind and below the pollen is located the stigma, a small hollow with a sticky surface to which pollen attaches when the pollen-bearing insect lands on the flower and, attracted by the honey guide, forces its way into the center looking for nectar. Upon leaving, that flower's pollen becomes stuck fast and is carried by the insect on to the next flower.

Sometimes the insect is attracted by the ingenious use of mimicry. A number of the European species of *Ophrys* have highly developed methods of affecting this. Their lips appear very lifelike, resembling the body of the bee, fly, or spider they wish to attract. Scent also plays a part in this deception, mimicking the female. In one species the flowering time is crucial, the beelike flower opening just three weeks before the female bees emerge, at a time when the males are already on the wing. Searching for the elusive mate, the male bee believes he has found the real thing and attempts copulation. This interaction between the flower and insect is a finely tuned relationship, where in some cases both are dependent on each other for their continued existence, but in this instance, the bee receives no reward.

There are other quite startling examples of this dependency among the tropical orchids, in which rewards are offered. Madagascar is the home of *Angraecum sesquipedale*, sometimes called the comet orchid, owing to the extra-long spur that is a nectar-holding, tubelike extension at the back of the lip. Its specific name means "a foot and a half," referring to the length of this spur, at the bottom of which is tempting nectar, accessible only to a single species of moth. When this orchid was discovered in the mid-nineteenth century, Charles Darwin predicted that an as-yet unknown species of hawkmoth with a proboscis the length of the spur must exist, otherwise the orchid would never be pollinated. It was much later, and some time after his death, that the moth was eventually found with a proboscis long enough to reach the nectar. In an allusion to Darwin's prediction, the moth was subsequently named *Xanthopan morgani praedicta*.

Fragrance also plays an important part in attracting pollinators to orchid flowers. Many of the epiphytic species are deliciously scented, a good enough reason on its own to cultivate them. *Oncidium ornithorynchum, Coelogyne ochracea, Maxillaria picta,* and *Encyclia radiata* are a few of the best examples. However, these orchids are not fragrant for twenty-four hours a day. Depending on when the pollinator is on the wing, some orchids are scented only at night, as with *Brassavola nodosa* and many species of *Angraecum*, which make use of night-flying moths. Others produce their scent earlier or later in the day, or only when the sun is shining, while on dull, rainy days the fragrance is nonexistent. Scent also wanes as the flower ages. Not all fragrances are sweet; some orchids make use of carrion flies and smell of rotting meat; these strange plants with grotesque flowers are found among the bulbophyllums. While the strongest fragrance persists in the species, a number of primary hybrids retain some degree of scent, but most often in the complex hybrids, all traces of scent are

The flowers of slipper orchids differ in their structure from most other types in that their lip is modified into a pouch (shown above left in *Phragmipedium* Eric Young). They also have two anthers, one on either side of the rostellum (equivalent to the column), and therefore two exits for the pollinating insect.

usually lost. Miltoniopsis and cattleyas are exceptions, and the modern hybrids, many times removed from the original species, are still sweetly scented, making them even more desirable to the collector.

Most orchid flowers are bisexual, containing both male and female organs, but separate male and female flowers are occasionally produced. In catasetums and cynoches, these are notably different in size and color, leading the early taxonomists to believe they were dealing with two separate species.

Seed and mycorrhiza

When an orchid has been fertilized by a pollinating insect, the stem immediately behind the flower, which contains the ovaries, begins to swell. Eventually, after a period of a few to nine months, it develops into a pear- or oval-shaped seed capsule, by which time the flower itself has dried and shriveled up. The seed capsule may contain anything up to a million minute seeds that, collectively, are a beautiful pale yellow and resemble fine sawdust. Studied under a microscope, it can be seen that each seed is encased in what appears to be a string bag.

In the wild, the seed is wind-blown. As the capsule ripens, it splits along longitudinal seams to release the seed a little at a time, over a period of days, to be carried away on the air currents. Of the tens of thousands of seeds released, only a very small amount (less than one percent) will germinate and grow. The extremely low germination rate is a result of the seeds' dependency on mycorrhiza, a microfungus that in turn needs the seed in order to survive. This dependency is not unique to orchids, for many plants and trees have a symbiotic relationship with their own mycorrhiza. Only those orchid seeds lucky enough to land where their specific mycorrhiza already exists have a chance of surviving. This is likely to be an area where the orchid is already established, cohabiting with the fungus. Once endowed, the mycorrhiza infects the seed and the two develop their symbiotic relationship, each becoming dependent on the other for their continued existence. In time, the mycorrhiza is confined to the orchid's roots and the surrounding area. In cultivation, the seed is harvested before coming into contact with the air and is kept sterile until it is immediately sown in glass containers on a growing medium (see page 214).

Once an orchid flower has been pollinated, it collapses and dies, while the stem behind the flower swells to form the seed capsule, seen here on *Encyclia cochleata*. It takes several months for the capsule to ripen, after which it splits along vertical ridges and the seed trickles out to be carried away on the wind. Note the shriveled remains of flowers below the capsules.

CYMBIDIUM LOWIANUM

CYMBIDIUM LOWIANUM var. CONCOLOR, Rolfe.

Cymbidium lowianum (far left) is an Indian species discovered in Myanmar (then Burma) in 1877. It has been responsible for the start of long breeding lines that have led to today's large green *Cymbidium* hybrids, such as C. Valley Blush 'Magnificent' (right).

Cymbidium lowianum var. *concolor* (left) is a naturally occurring variant in that the red band on the lip has been replaced by yellow, creating further variation in its hybrids. It was first described in 1891.

Species and hybrids

An orchid species has two parts to its Latin name, the first being the generic or genus name, for example *Cymbidium*. The second element is the specific epithet that distinguishes one species from another, i.e. *lowianum*. A species is a wild, naturally occurring plant with usually little or no difference between individuals, called clones. Occasionally, however, sufficient variation does appear, with distinct flower coloration, size, or markings to justify a varietal name being given to the specific clone, such as *Cymbidium lowianum* var. *concolor*. So there exist species and their variations which can, over millions of years, evolve into separate species in their own right, and many orchids are still actively evolving today. Where separate populations of related species exist in the wild in close proximity, sharing the same pollinator, there arises the opportunity for cross-pollination between them, thus creating a natural hybrid. However, these occurrences are quite unusual in nature, and the resulting hybrids generally will not go on to breed further. Termed mules, they appear to be incapable of further reproduction.

Hybrids are more usually the result of a grower, or breeder, deliberately crossing two different species together; the first cross produces a primary hybrid. Further generations of breeding can achieve intergeneric hybrids, where specimens of related genera are crossed together. In this way orchids have achieved a far greater degree of hybridizing than has proved possible in any other plant family, greatly extending the range of plants and, in most instances, providing enhanced color, size, and general appeal. In the last 150 years since the first hybrids were produced, over 100,000 orchid hybrids have been officially registered, with about another 3,000 new ones being added each year.

The process of hybridizing

By the mid-nineteenth century, orchids held a high horticultural profile. Early hybridizing experiments created great excitement, and there appeared to be no difficulty in obtaining vast quantities of seed. While seed was plentiful and could be produced with comparative ease from such diverse orchids as the British terrestrials and the tropical epiphytes, achieving germination proved to be far more difficult. At a time when the symbiotic association with mycorrhiza was unknown, it was not fully understood why so few seeds germinated. The early method of sowing was to sprinkle seed over the surface of the potting mixture in which an adult plant was growing, or to use seedling pots prepared with growing medium taken from the pot of an already established plant. Some measure of success was gained in this way, but all too frequently it was short-lived, as the few seedlings grown did not survive their first winter, and most succumbed to rot.

In 1847, the Reverend and Honourable W. Herbert, Dean of Manchester Cathedral, in England, had moderate success with raising hybrids and he wrote, "Cross-breeding among orchidaceous plants would perhaps lead to very startling results, but unfortunately they are not easily raised from seed . . . ." Ten years later, in 1856, the first orchid hybrid was officially recognized and recorded. This was *Calanthe* Dominyi, produced at the nursery of James Veitch & Sons of Exeter, Devon, in southwest England, and named in honor of the raiser, John Dominy, their head orchid grower. This achievement was the result of discussions between John Dominy and John Harris, a local surgeon who had studied the orchid on frequent visits to the nursery. He suggested to Dominy a method of pollinating the orchid flower, and seedlings of different genera were subsequently raised. Dominy's first venture was with cattleyas, but the few that survived took six years to flower. His initial success was therefore the calanthe, a cross between *C. masuca* and *C. furcata*, which bloomed within three years of germinating.

At this time new species were still being discovered, and as each bloomed, it was named and described by one of the eminent botanists of the day.

Calanthe Veitchii (right) was one of the earliest hybrids to appear (1859), and the first to gain a first class certificate from the Royal Horticultural Society in Britain.

Laeliocattleya Drumbeat (left) is a modern-day clone descended from the bigeneric hybrid genus (*Laelia* × *Cattleya*) first made in 1887.

Veitch therefore took his *Calanthe* Dominyi hybrid to Dr. Lindley at the Royal Botanic Gardens at Kew in Britain, who described it as he would a new species, latinizing the hybrid name. Dr. Lindley, perhaps realizing the future consequences of such an event, exclaimed, "Why, you will drive the botanists mad!" Perplexed by many of the discoveries that the botanists were revealing, Dr. Lindley went on to remark in the following year, "What with heteranthism [having some sterile flowers on an inflorescence], dimorphism [having both male and female flowers on an inflorescence], pelorism [having abnormal flowers, where the lip features are transformed onto the petals], and hybridism, our favorite orchids may be found to assume as many disguises as an actor."

Once the hybridizing of orchids had been shown to be moderately successful, all the major growers started to dabble in raising seedlings. The five surviving cattleyas raised at Veitch's nursery eventually flowered, gaining significant recognition. Then, in 1859, *Calanthe* Veitchii appeared, a deciduous hybrid from a cross between *C. rosea* and *C. vestita*. This beautiful plant became the first *Calanthe* hybrid to receive a first class certificate from the Royal Horticultural Society. Still widely grown today, it is a testimony to the great age that orchids can attain.

Further hybrids appeared in all the popular genera. The first *Paphiopedilum* (then *Cypripedium*) hybrid raised in 1869 was named *Paphiopedilum* Harrisianum after the Exeter surgeon. The names were originally latinized in the same way as those of orchid species, which in later years caused considerable confusion as, by their names, hybrids could not be distinguished from the species. At this time Britain was the world leader in orchid hybridizing, but it was soon taken up by other growers in Europe. Intergeneric hybrids also started appearing; in 1904 the first *Odontioda* (*Odontoglossum* × *Cochlioda*) was registered, raised by Charles Vuylsteke of Ghent in Belgium. It was called *Odontioda* Vuylstekeae (see page 29) and its red coloring caused a sensation when shown to the Royal Horticultural Society. It was awarded a first class certificate and a silver-gilt Lindley Medal. Vuylsteke was also responsible for creating the genus so popular today, *Vuylstekeara*. Indeed, one of the most successful orchids of

Paphiopedilum Harrisianum (below) was the first *Paphiopedilum* hybrid raised, flowering in 1869. It was named for John Harris, the surgeon who suggested how orchids could be pollinated.

5375.

W.Fitch, del et lith.

Vincent Brooks, Imp.

Vuylstekeara **is a genus created by Charles Vuylsteke by crossing** *Cochlioda* **x** *Miltonia* **x** *Odontoglossum.* ***V.* Cambria 'Plush' (left), first raised in 1936, is its most popular descendant.**

all time is *Vuylstekeara* Cambria 'Plush' FCC/RHS, raised in 1936 and today seen more widely than ever.

Another great name of the nineteenth century in orchids was that of Frederick Sander; so prolific were the new species he introduced into cultivation that they earned him the title of the "Orchid King." Shelley wrote of him in the satire magazine *Punch*, "Frederick Sander the Orchid King, is filling all his boxes for export in the spring." Sander realized that the new hybrids were becoming numerous and that, unless some record was kept of the parentage of each plant, chaos would ensue in the horticultural world. In 1901 he started an orchid register, recording every hybrid made to date, and asking hybridizers to notify him of each cross they flowered, with details of the name, parentage, and date of flowering. The list was a great success and has continued to the present day, retaining the name "Sander's List of Orchid Hybrids." Several volumes were produced up to 1947, after which hybrids were becoming so numerous that a new volume was added every five years, and currently every three years. Since it was started, over 100,000 hybrids have been registered. In the 1960s, the Royal Horticultural Society took over the production from the Sander family, and the list remains the sole register for orchid hybrids worldwide. Six times a year, the new hybrids coming into registration appear in *The Orchid Review* and subsequently in various leading orchid journals around the world. Today the system is computerized and available on CD-ROM.

Since the first tentative steps in hybridizing, orchids have proved to be very promiscuous, with the result that many multigeneric hybrids are now routinely produced. Long breeding lines have become established, often with the resulting progeny bearing little, or no, resemblance to the original species. Owing to the foresight of Frederick Sander, it is possible to trace any modern hybrid back through many generations of hybridizing, and more than 100 years, to the original species. Orchids share this achievement of complete breeding lines only with racehorses. But whereas any registered thoroughbred horse can be traced back to just three Arabian stallions, individual orchids trace back their ancestry to a much wider species base.

Raising orchids from seed

The raising of orchids from seed remained commercially unviable until the early years of the twentieth century, when Dr. Noel Bernard, a French scientist, devised a way of identifying the microfungus that existed in the roots of adult plants and of isolating it under laboratory conditions. By inoculating the seed

Odontioda **Vuylstekeae FCC/RHS (right) was the first hybrid between the genera** *Cochlioda* **and** *Odontoglossum.* **Raised in 1904, it was named for Charles Vuylsteke, the Belgian nurseryman and hybridizer. It is shown here with its parents,** *Odontoglossum crispum* **and** *Cochlioda noezliana,* **in an illustration taken from Curtis's** *Botanical Magazine.*

M.S.del, J.N.Fitch lith.   Vincent Brooks Day & Son, Ld Imp

with this, he took the problem of poor germination away from the grower and he solved it scientifically. This was the first, but not the last, time that science would come to the aid of orchid growers. In 1906, Dr. Bernard published his results, which were at that time a revelation, and by the 1920s, the English firm of Charlesworth & Co. had begun raising seedlings commercially by his method. This nursery specialized in odontoglossums and, as soon as it became apparent that specific orchids each had their own mycorrhiza, they were able to isolate the odontoglossum fungus and use this living mycelium to grow orchid seedlings symbiotically. Using laboratory flasks, they inserted a jelly medium upon which they had injected the mycelium and the seed; this was done under sterile conditions to prevent contamination. The results were astounding; because the seedlings spent their first year in the flasks, they grew more strongly and were better able to survive when placed into community pots on conventional growing medium.

A few years later,

Sanderara Rippon Tor 'Burnham' (right) is one of the many clones in the trigeneric genus (Odontoglossum x Cochlioda x Brassia) named after the famous nurseryman, Frederick Sander.

in the mid-1920s, Dr. Knutson, a scientist working at the University of California, developed a method of bypassing the natural mycorrhiza by substituting it for the basic trace elements known to exist within the fungus. He produced an artificial formula that, when combined with the base media, provided an ideal germinating ground for the seed. His famous formula "C," for which he originally charged $800, became the basis for all seed sowing throughout the world once it

was widely publicized. Orchids today are still raised in the same way, with modifications to the basic formula. It is now possible to purchase various seed-sowing kits, and the technique has become so simplified that it is within the reach of all amateur growers who wish to raise their own seedlings (see page 213).

Paphiopedilum Gina Short (left) is a modern-day hybrid bred from *P. delenatii*, the first pink-flowered species discovered in Vietnam nearly a century ago.

Latest discoveries

By the end of the nineteenth century, all the known desirable tropical orchids were in cultivation, and it was assumed there was little of much interest left to find. The popular genera had all been classified, and hybridizing among them had begun, with the best of the new crosses creating as much excitement as had been previously reserved for recently discovered species. Many more orchids still existed in the wild but these were less attractive types, referred to as "botanicals" and of interest to only a few.

There remained, however, vast tracts of land unexplored by westerners. China was still closed to outsiders and Indochina, now Vietnam, was under French occupation. In 1913, a French soldier returned to his country from service in Vietnam carrying a small plant in his rucksack. This turned out to be a beautiful, pink-flowered *Paphiopedilum*, of an undescribed species, and a rare find indeed. The plant was cultivated at the nursery of Vacherot & Lecoufle, near Paris, which successfully flowered it and later raised it from seed, subsequently selling seedlings around the world. The plant was *Paphiopedilum delenatii*, and it produced a number of highly sought-after hybrids, bringing pink coloring into the genus for the first time. At the close of the twentieth century, Vietnam is a country at peace once again and a more relaxed attitude has seen it open to western botanists. As a result, nearly 100 years later, new populations of *Paphiopedilum delenatii* have been discovered and brought into cultivation, greatly widening the gene bank and offering new possibilities for breeding.

The latter half of the twentieth century has also provided the orchid world with some extraordinary new discoveries in paphiopedilums. Between 1984 and 1986, the orchid world was stunned by the exquisite beauty of four

Phragmipedium beeseae (right) is an important modern discovery, found in Peru in 1981. Bringing red into the genus for the first time, it sparked off a new range of hybrids, creating further generations of unique orchids.

previously unknown plants from China: *P. armeniacum*, with pure gold flowers unique in the genus; *P. emersonii*, a large-petaled, white flower with a pale yellow pouch; *P. malipoense*, contrasting delicate green, purple-veined petals with a bulbous pouch on a tall stem; and *P. micranthum*, a light green and pink flower with an extremely bulbous pink pouch. As these plants have come into cultivation, they have been justly recognized and showered with awards from the United States, Britain, South Africa, and Australia. While the species have proved to be challenging to cultivate, their progeny, when crossed with more vigorous types, have grown and flowered readily. Immediately following their discovery, huge quantities were shipped around the world, but within a short time this export was banned, and it is unlikely that further wild specimens will be acquired outside China. It is therefore important to cherish those plants already in cultivation, to maintain a lasting stock of these beautiful orchids.

Peru is a country that has been extensively explored for many years, yet here, in 1981, a further sensational orchid, *Phragmipedium besseae*, was discovered with such stunning, bright red flowers that it is hard to understand how it came to be overlooked for so long. In fact, the plant grows on extremely inaccessible cliff faces high in the Andes, invisible from the ground and only reachable by helicopter, which is how the plants were collected. Once it became known, entire colonies poured into cultivation, begging the question whether it had been made extinct in the wild. But in cultivation *P. besseae* has proved to be easy to raise from seed, so the species should not be difficult to conserve. Natural habitats are not always safe places for orchids in the modern world, where so much is under threat of destruction, whereas in cultivation, the plants often have a better chance of survival.

Prior to the discovery of *P. besseae*, all *Phragmipedium* hybrids were created around the turn of the nineteenth century, but it was found that after only one or two generations the plants became sterile, and no further breeding could be done with them. However, by the time *P. besseae* came on the scene, there was a better understanding of genetics, enabling chromosome numbers to be counted and manipulated in order to give a greater degree of fertility. This is an area of new breeding possibilities that has yet to reach its full potential and that is eagerly awaited in the orchid world.

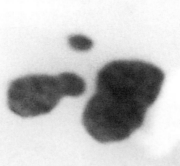

Part One
Origins

from origins to cultiv

Orchids, more than any other plant, have adapted and modified their features to enable species to take advantage of every possible environment on earth. Opportunists, they are equally at home in forests, grasslands, and swamps, as in deserts and other drought-ridden areas where they endure searing heat and freezing cold. They are found from shorelines to mountain ranges, clinging to inaccessible rock faces or to the extremities of tiny twigs. They thrive on branches high in the tree canopy or on the trunks below, and on the ground they fight for earthly survival among tall grasses. Indeed, only the grasses are as widespread and abundant as orchids, but they are confined to terrestrial habitation.

Vanilla pompona (left) is a native of tropical South America, where it inhabits forested areas, scrambling vinelike through the trees.

Diverse habitats

Experts in survival, orchids are the most durable and toughest of all flowering plants. They have exploited the most unlikely situations, spreading away from the warmer environs of the equator to within the edges of the harsh arctic regions of Russia and Alaska in the north and to the extremities of the great land masses of South America and Australia to the south. Their adaptability is legendary. For example, in the tropical regions stretching from Africa and Madagascar to South America and the West Indies there exists a curious orchid that scrambles through the tree branches to climb high into the canopy on long vinelike stems. Here its leaves are thick and fleshy, its roots only occasionally extending down to the ground. This is the vanilla (*V. pompona*) whose pods give the flavoring for culinary use. Other species of vanilla, however, such as *V. humboltii*, grow in desert conditions, creeping along at ground level where their leaves are reduced to tiny leaf bracts with short

In the tropical rain forests (right), some orchids grow as terrestrials, living in the leaf litter at the foot of huge forest trees.

Since the discovery of orchids over 200 years ago, plant hunters searched mountains and forests all over the world to bring back new species for collectors. *Coelogyne cristata* (below) was found growing on the trunks and thick branches of trees high in the mountains of Nepal, where it can assume huge proportions over many years.

and stunted roots, relying instead upon the fleshy stems to retain sufficient moisture for survival. The vanilla was originally grown by the Aztecs of South America for its flavoring and was introduced into Europe by the Spanish conquistador Cortés, in the sixteenth century. Today, vanilla is the only orchid grown as a commercial crop for its fruits, the dried seedpods from which vanilla extract is obtained. The flowers are mostly large and showy, yellow or green, but they are individually very short-lived, often flowering for less than twenty-four hours. In cultivation, vanillas are shy-flowerers until they become very large and are given full sun, when flowering becomes almost continuous.

Along the coast and estuaries of Venezuela and spreading through the islands of the West Indies are vast mangrove swamps, a muddy saltwater environment that would seem an unlikely place to find orchids; but here, too, one notable species has made its home. Growing on the mangrove trees and shrubs just above the high-water mark lives the showy *Caulathron bicornatum*. The plant is also unusual because it has hollow pseudobulbs that, as they mature, develop small splits at the base, encouraging a species of fireant to enter and produce their colony inside. This association clearly provides some form of protection for both orchid and insect but it would also have made collecting the plants extremely hazardous. The plant is in cultivation, however, and has been used sparingly in hybridization, its showy white flowers adding grace to its progeny. Other salt-tolerant orchids can be found off the coasts of Thailand and Malaysia, where sheer-sided limestone cliffs and sea stacks rise vertically from the water. Here, in the most inaccessible of places, a slipper orchid, *Paphiopedilum bellatulum*, clings with scant roots to the rock faces, apparently unaffected by the constant drenchings of saltwater.

Cypripedium calceolus (left) is a lovely European terrestrial slipper orchid, tolerating extremely cold temperatures on snow-covered hillsides. It is now almost extinct in the wild, though attempts have been made to reintroduce it at protected sites.

Calanthe triplicata is a terrestrial orchid growing up to a meter (3 feet) tall. It has a wide distribution through India, Southeast Asia, Indonesia, Japan, and Australia.

In temperate climates, terrestrial orchids (such as species of *Epipactis*) grow happily in sand dunes close to the sea. Alaska and Russia can boast tundra-growing orchids (species of *Cypripedium* and *Planthera*), little plants that grow and flower in the short summer season while the ground is free from snow. While these are some of the more extreme habitats occupied by orchids, the majority are found in less dramatic situations. Every continent and island has its indigenous orchid populations but, as we have seen, the equatorial regions hold the main treasure trove of orchid species.

The home environment

Orchids that exist in extreme conditions around the world are not generally those found in cultivation. Their specialist culture would not produce the rewards expected by enthusiasts, who prefer to grow orchids with the largest, showiest, and most colorful blooms. These species of orchid and the many hybrids raised from them can, for the purpose of growing them at home, be divided into three main cultural categories, determined by the environment in which they grow in the wild. The main categories of cool-, intermediate-, and warm-growing orchids are more fully explored in the following three chapters.

Cool-growing orchids include those that live at high altitudes in the wild, such as *Cymbidium*, *Odontoglossum*, and some dendrobiums, as well as *Encyclia* and *Coelogyne*. The first three are readily available in a multitude of hybrids encompassing the entire color range, while the smaller-growing encyclias and some coelogynes are ideal where space is limited. They all will grow well indoors, provided they are not exposed to excesses of temperature such as will occur in a sunroom that can easily overheat in summer. Likewise, these orchids will not thrive in an area left unheated during the winter. Choose a well-lit part of a living room that is not directly in the sun; it needs to be

Phalaenopsis (right) have become today's top indoor flowering orchid. The almost constant temperature of a centrally heated home suits these warm-growing orchids well, providing conditions close to those they enjoy in the wild.

warm by day and cool at night. Intermediate orchids include the fabulous tropical American cattleyas, as well as warmer-growing slipper orchids and *Miltoniopsis*. Grow the exotic cattleyas in a warm room with good light, where some background heating can be left on overnight in winter. Slipper orchids and miltoniopsis need a slightly shadier position to protect them from direct sun.

The warmest-growing of all the popular varieties are *Phalaenopsis*. These moth orchids originate from the hotter environments found at lower elevations in the forested tropics of Asia and Malaysia. With their wide, fleshy leaves and their tendency to make aerial roots, they need a warm but shady position, where they can be kept constantly moist. They also require warm nighttime temperatures, but should not be placed too close to a heat source, such as a radiator, which would dehydrate them.

Having selected a position for each plant that corresponds most closely to its natural environment, you can set up a small growing area consisting of a humidity tray filled with pebbles. Maintain moisture by keeping the pebbles damp, watering the orchids regularly, and spraying lightly when possible. Provided their basic cultural needs are met, more specialized treatment can be given for individual orchid groups (see the introduction to each genus in A Collection of Orchids).

The discovery of orchids

Two hundred years ago, tropical epiphytic orchids were unknown in the western world. The British Empire was spreading across the globe and the vast areas of South America and Southeast Asia were reached by large sailing ships whose masters were intent on discovery. These sea captains were the first to return with fabulous treasures from such partially uncharted lands. A few orchid specimens seem to have reached England in this way during the eighteenth century, but did not survive for long and attracted little attention. They were wrongly thought to be parasitic plants, a misconception that lingers to the present day.

The first tropical epiphytic orchid to flower in Britain was described in 1763 as *Epidendrum cochleatum* (now *Encyclia cochleata*) and, not being as eye-catching as later introductions, was considered a mere curiosity. The generic name, *Epidendrum*, meant "upon a tree," which was all the information then available for classification purposes; *cochleatum* referred to the shell-like appearance of the lip. As further plants followed and were subsequently described, it soon became apparent that they could not all be of the same genus, and separate classifications were established. Before the botanists of the day realized they were dealing with such a vast and diverse family of plants, the huge task of describing and naming the various orchid species had begun.

If the first importations were of curiosity value and did little to fire the imagination, later discoveries held all the promise of a horticultural revolution. In the early part of the nineteenth century, William Cattley, a noted British horticulturist, received a consignment of non-orchidaceous plants

Pub. April 1 1791 by W Curtis St Georges Crescent.

Encyclia fragrans (above) came into cultivation alongside *E. cochleata*, under the name *Epidendrum*. One of the first orchids to be grown, it was described in 1788.

from South America, wrapped in what appeared to be a bundle of dried sticks. Cattley noticed that some of these sticks were green and appeared to be alive. He placed them on one side and these "dead" sticks produced new growth, one of which eventually blossomed, with bright rose-purple flowers of such size and beauty it astounded those who saw it. The plant was described by John Lindley in 1821 as *Cattleya labiata*. This species and its hybrids are still among the most flamboyant and highly prized of all orchids today. This specimen alone was enough to excite the passions of the horticulturists and to inspire a longing that led to greed, envy and deception and to huge fortunes being paid for the finest plants.

In large country estates at this time, gardens and parklands were being developed and land-scaped, and interest in all Asian plants and trees was intense. In society, horticulture held a very high profile, the like of which we have not seen since, and as each new introduction arrived, excitement mounted. A lucrative trade was begun by a few nurserymen who sent orchid collectors to follow the earlier explorers to South America, as well as to India, Nepal, and neighboring countries to scour the Andes and the Himalayas, where orchids were known to grow. They traveled inland, often into unexplored and dangerous territory, and found many new species growing in trees at high altitudes, where the climate was cool and moist, and drying breezes cleared away the early morning mists.

These plants were brought down from the high mountain areas to the head of the nearest river, here to start their long journey by boat to the docks, where they were piled high before being packed into boxes to await transportation by sailing ship to England. The sea journey could take up to six weeks, at a time before the steam packets operated a faster service. When the cargo arrived at British ports, steam trains carried the plants to the nurseries where at last the boxes were opened. All too often, excitement turned to despair when the stench of rotting vegetation accompanied the opening of the lids, and the majority of plants were found to have died en route or been devoured by rats or cockroaches. However, if just a few survived, this justified orders for more plants to be sent, in the belief that

Cattleya labiata (right) was the first of the showy cattleyas to be discovered, causing a sensation in 1821 when it flowered for the first time.

there was an endless supply of orchids in the rain forests—such had become the desire to own the latest horticultural adornments. It will never be known how many orchids perished in this way, some of them new to science and lost before being described. Frequent shipwrecks also accounted for innumerable losses.

The first plants to survive the rigors of travel were placed in hot and steamy "stove" houses, for it was thought that all the orchids had come from the lowland forest areas and would therefore grow in these dark and airless places. Not until information regarding their true habitats was relayed back by collectors were better constructions erected for the orchids. The first glasshouses were iron structures with small panes of glass which gave more light, and ventilators to allow fresh air to reach the plants, creating better growing conditions. Very few of these huge structures, designed for botanical gardens and private estates, remain today.

Mastery of the conditions under which the tropical orchids would grow soon led to an even greater demand for plants, and there was jealousy among growers over the best and the newest. Orchid hunters were under pressure to find new species and would stop at little to prevent their rivals from getting to a site first. The nurserymen were also known to deliberately falsify the location of a new discovery, claiming it to have been found many miles from its true location, to prevent competition. There were also reports of plants being burnt rather than left for another to find. It was not unknown for a collector, on reaching his goal, to strip the area of every plant, taking away only the biggest and best specimens for which there was a ready market at home. All

smaller pieces and seedlings would be destroyed on the spot, enabling the collector to inform his employer that he had all the available plants. This may also account for the massive specimens grown in collections during that era. The growers had the pick of the finest plants as well as the rarest of species which are, in many cases, now gone.

The orchid hunters

Orchid hunting was a dangerous business at a time when vast tracts of land were occupied by native peoples who did not always welcome intruders. Several collectors lost their lives, often in suspicious circumstances, either at the hands of the local inhabitants or by succumbing to

The splendid *Miltoniopsis roezlii* (left) was discovered in 1873 and named for Benedict Roezl, who discovered it in Colombia. Originally described as *Odontoglossum*, it was later transferred to *Miltonia* and, more recently, to its present genus, *Miltoniopsis*.

Vanda Violeta 'Fuchs Sky' (above) is a modern descendant of the legendary blue orchid of Myanmar, *Vanda coerulea* (right). The species was discovered in what was then called Burma in 1837, but it was not until 1850 that large consignments of living plants reached England, having been collected in the Khasi Hills.

tropical diseases from which they had no immunity. Others simply disappeared into the dense virgin forest, never to be seen again.

Most of these men were young adventurers driven on by the prospect of fame and riches. Such a man was Benedict Roezl, who left his native Prague in the Czech Republic to spend over forty years in the tropics between about 1830 and 1870. As a young man, he had lost an arm through an accident with a jute-crushing machine, and he found the iron hook that he wore in place of a hand very useful in tearing plants from the trees. Roezl discovered about 800 plants new to science, not all orchids, and shipped them to England in such astronomical numbers that they were measured by weight. One consignment of orchids weighed eight tons and another, containing both orchids and cacti, ten tons. Orchids named after him include *Pleurothallis roezlii*, *Miltonia roezlii*, and *Masdevallia roezlii*. Today a statue of him stands in Prague, holding a cattleya flower in his hand.

Sir Joseph Hooker, an eminent botanist from the Royal Botanic Gardens at Kew in England, led plant-hunting expeditions in the Khasi Hills of northern India in the early part of the nineteenth century. Here, at an altitude of over 1,000 meters (3,000–4,000 feet) on a cold, windswept grassland where stunted oak trees grew, he encountered the beautiful, elusive blue-colored *Vanda coerulea* growing in profusion on the bare, lichen-free branches. He had the trees stripped of their ethereal treasures and carted away by manual labor; these plants were measured in "men's loads," and it took seven men to carry them all. It was later reported that very few had reached England alive and the remnants were sold at auction for between £3 and £10 each. A later expedition to the same region was mounted by William Micholitz, a German who collected for Frederick Sander. He reported finding *Vanda coerulea* growing on rocky outcrops and trees exposed to the full sun during the day and experiencing very cold nights that left them covered in hoar frost. The fabled blue vanda obviously thrived in this extremely harsh environment, with its wide variations in temperature.

On the other side of the world another orchid rarity had come to light in 1857. This was *Dendrobium schroderianum*, named after Baron Schröder, an important orchid collector. Although known, its natural whereabouts remained a mystery until Frederick Sander sent one of his collectors to search for it in New Guinea. Micholitz was in the company of natives when he ventured into the nearby forest to be confronted by trees festooned with the elusive dendrobium. Having cabled back to Sander news of his good fortune, he loaded a large boat with his acquisitions with help from the natives. But before the ship set sail, fire broke out and every plant was lost. Once again Micholitz searched for *Dendrobium schroderianum*, and this time he found plants growing not upon trees, but on human remains in a native graveyard, where it was the custom to place the finest plant specimens among the bleached bones of the dead. Offerings of beads, mirrors, and, finally, a roll of copper wire secured him the dendrobium growing upon a human skull, but there was a condition: If the skull was to be removed, it must be accompanied on its journey by two sacred idols to ensure that no harm should come to the family's ancestor. The orchid duly arrived in England and was auctioned, still attached to its skull, along with the accompanying idols.

In *Ascoenda* Fuchs Yellow Snow (left), raised in Florida in 1991, the *Ascoenda* influence is almost erased by breeding, leaving a *Vanda* (*Eulanthe*) *sanderiana*-type bloom, its color and patterning clearly visible on the lower sepals.

Early nurserymen

The costly excursions of the adventurous orchid hunters were paid for by the first orchid nurserymen. By the early years of the nineteenth century, several nurseries in London were dealing in orchids, one of the best-known being Conrad Loddiges & Sons of Hackney, which employed several collectors to meet the growing demand for these tropical plants. James Veitch, a Scot, started his own nursery in Exeter in southwest England and in 1808 employed the Lobb brothers to collect orchids, along with other plants and trees. Hugh Low started a nursery in London, later moving it to the country; it remained in business until the 1960s and was known for such new introductions as *Cymbidium lowianum*.

As we have seen (page 28), one of the greatest of the early commercial nurserymen was Frederick Sander, known as the "Orchid King." He started his business in 1860, mainly through his friendship with Benedict Roezl, who collected for him. By 1894, Sander had nurseries operating in Bruges and New York, but the most imposing was in Saint Albans, Hertfordshire, where sixty

PL. 124.

J.Nugent Fitch del.et lith   VANDA SANDERIANA.   B.S.Williams Publ.

Eulanthe sanderiana (above) is the only species in this genus, closely related to Vanda, with which it will interbreed. Introduced from the Philippines in 1882, it was named for Frederick Sander, the "Orchid King."

large greenhouses occupied four acres of land. The nursery had its own railway siding, bringing visitors and new plants alike directly into the establishment, and kings and queens were among those who stepped off the train into a baronial hall that led to the greenhouses. A special display house enabled visitors to view the orchids in a natural setting created by a rock garden, where waterfalls plunged down into rock pools. At its height, the nursery had a staff of several hundreds and it survived through three generations of the family name.

The early nurseries relied on a huge workforce to keep their establishments running. They required boiler men, stokers, carpenters, and an army of apprentices to fetch and carry for the craftsmen. Of all the workers, those who held the position of greatest esteem were the orchid growers, who underwent rigorous training before being employed by one of the large estates. The growers were responsible for plants that had cost their owner far more than they would pay their employees in a year. There was also a steady supply of youngsters keen to work and learn a skill, and each one gaining employment would be assigned to a grower. An important part of their duties was to polish the brass door handles on the greenhouses each morning and sweep away puddles in constant readiness for visitors. It would be several years before the young trainee would be permitted to handle the valuable orchids. Orchid nurseries were also beginning to operate outside of Britain at this time, especially in Germany and Belgium, as well as in New England. The rest of the U.S. came into orchids later, however, during a more stable period following the Civil War.

Because of the dangers and high cost of transporting tropical orchids to England, and the losses regularly encountered, it was not surprising that the finest specimens fetched very high prices. New importations were largely sold at auction by one or two prominent firms of auctioneers whose weekly sales

attracted orchid fanciers and their growers. The most plentiful orchids had become almost commonplace and would sell cheaply, usually by the bundle. But when a new variety was first offered, the intense competition to own it resulted in unrealistically high prices being paid—in some cases over $100. This method of selling orchids remained unchanged for many years, with the last auctions dying out only in the mid-1900s. The nurseries then started to produce their first mail-order catalogs, often listing individual plants and giving their size and the number of pseudobulbs or growths. The larger establishments employed a watercolor artist to illustrate the flowers.

Exhibiting orchids

As major collections became established, orchids started to be displayed at horticultural exhibitions to which they were sent, carefully packed and in full bloom, even to extremely far-reaching destinations. In 1869, R.Warner sent fifty orchids to the International Horticultural Exhibition in Saint Petersburg in Russia—a journey that took eight days by train. The plants arrived in perfect condition and, after two weeks on display, were returned home; three weeks later, one well-traveled *Odontoglossum crispum* specimen was exhibited at the Royal Horticultural Society (RHS) in London, still in a prime state. These displays were, for the nurseries, a means of advertising their plants and, for the private growers, a way of gaining recognition in their field. In Britain, horticultural exhibitions were held mainly in London until the formation of the Manchester and North of England Orchid Society in 1897. This was the first amateur orchid society to be formed, and it became the forerunner of many more.

Both the RHS and the Manchester Society initiated a system of awards for the finest orchids and other societies throughout the world followed suit. These awards continue today and are recognized throughout the orchid-growing world as the pinnacle of achievement in both quality and breeding. The main categories are the Award of Merit (AM) and the First Class Certificate (FCC). Any plant receiving an award carries the appropriate letters after its name, as in *Miltoniopsis* Rouge 'California Plum' AM/AOS, which denotes an Award of Merit given by the American Orchid Society to the distinct clone named 'California Plum.' Awarded plants had to be given an additional clone name to distinguish them from other varieties of, in this case, Rouge, which may not necessarily receive an award. There is also a Certificate

of Cultural Commendation given to growers of exceptionally well-cultivated plants; this is the highest accolade that growers, and in particular amateurs, can receive.

In 1885, the first world orchid conference was held in London, England, and its proceedings were published. This period also saw the printing of two extremely beautiful books on orchids, published when color reproduction was a time-consuming and expensive operation. Such books had to be sponsored privately and copies sold at an exclusive price, a risky business even for a person of some means. James Bateman produced both *Odontoglossums* and *Orchids of Mexico*, both massive works printed on elephant folio depicting life-size orchids; today these rare books command the highest prices.

Following the formation in 1889 of the award-giving RHS Orchid Committee, it became necessary to record each awarded flower for reference and for later comparison with others. The only way of obtaining a true color likeness was by water-color reproduction, for which an artist was employed. This method of depiction is still preferred by many over that of photography, and the painting of orchid awards continues today, so that there now exists a complete record of award-holding orchids dating from 1897. The first artist to be engaged was Nellie Roberts, who started painting at the age of sixteen and continued with this task until she retired in 1953, having by then illustrated over 4,500 individual flowers.

The orchid industry

As the horticultural revolution taking place in Britain expanded into Europe, the first orchid establishments were created in Germany, Belgium, and Denmark. In France, a partnership was formed between Vacherot & Lecoufle, whose nurseries at Boissy Saint Léger near Paris soon commanded world attention; this is the oldest orchid business still in existence.

After the American Civil War, there followed a more stable period in the history of the U.S. Frederick Sander proved he was a man of vision by traveling to New England, where he was instrumental in setting up a number of commercial nurseries. By the early years of the twentieth century it had become apparent that the climate of California was perfect for horticulture and, once water supplies had been channeled and diverted, this desert state became the plant center of the U.S. Orchids were grown for the burgeoning cut-flower market and new varieties cultivated and brought to flowering in far less time than was possible in the colder climate of Britain. New nurseries appeared, growing orchid varieties outdoors under shade cloth, the plants bedded out over vast areas where they grew into huge specimens with the minimum of care and cost. Here, the cut-flower industry became more important than the hobby-plant trade, being led by the flagship nurseries of Armacost and Royston and by Gallop and Stribling.

The balmy climate of San Francisco also suited orchid growing, and here Rod McLellan set up his well-known nursery, Acres of Orchids. The town of Santa Barbara has become synonymous with orchids, and each year it hosts the nation's largest show. Florida's tropical climate favored the warmer-growing orchids, and this state has become a second center of excellence for the production of fine hybrids, with nurseries producing their own varieties beneath shade cloth without the expense of winter heating. While in the East orchid cultivation was practiced by the ancient Chinese 2,000 years ago, today

Sophrocattlaelia **Thisbe (above) is an example of an early award-winning orchid hybrid painted by Nellie Roberts around 1910. She was the first artist employed by the Royal Horticultural Society to record every awarded plant.**

the center has shifted to Japan, where many new hybrids are registered. The largest orchid show in the world, attended by huge numbers, is staged annually in Tokyo.

Within a few short years of the death of Queen Victoria in 1901, the world was at war; even after 1918, world stability was short-lived and within another twenty years, war had broken out once again. Fearful that the best of the British *Cymbidium*, *Cattleya*, and *Cypripedium* (*Paphiopedilum*) hybrids would not survive, the best stud plants were sold to eager buyers in the U.S. and Australia, throwing open the expanding industry to other countries. The war years in Britain were immediately followed by one of the worst winters of the century, at a time when fuel for heating orchids was unobtainable. It was therefore not until the 1950s that seedlings were once again being raised in Britain in significant enough numbers to meet the increasing worldwide market. Much of Britain's earlier success was attributable to one plant, *Cymbidium* Alexanderi 'Westonbirt' FCC/RHS, which had flowered for the first time in 1922. This plant proved to be a superior clone, with extra chromosomes causing it to be an outstanding parent and producing progeny with flowers of excellent quality, possessing all the qualities desired by breeders.

The new orchid hybrids then being developed were to satisfy the increasing numbers of amateur growers. The awakening interest by enthusiasts led to the emergence of amateur orchid societies whose common theme was the organization of local conferences and shows. Around this time, commercial nurseries formed the British Orchid Growers' Association, to gain combined stability and recognition, and for over forty years presented the most prestigious orchid show in London. Now under the auspices of the RHS and named the London Orchid Show, it is traditionally held in March, the prime time for the flowering of the popular orchids that make up the majority of the exhibits.

The rich coloring of the lip and the exquisite patterning on the petals of this fine hybrid, *Phalaenopsis San Luca* (right), have been achieved through the dedication of modern hybridizers, in this case in California.

Millions of seedlings had long been shipped from Britain to all around the world, until regulations coming into force from various countries restricted this trade. In particular, because of the fear of spreading the *Cymbidium* mosaic virus which appeared in British-bred plants, Australia and New Zealand banned all importation which, in due course, led to the development of their own hybrids. While the focus was now on the newest hybrids, which were constantly improving, there remained a demand for wild-collected species, although on nothing like the scale that had existed during the previous century. In 1973, many states signed the Washington Convention on International Trade in Endangered Species (CITES), designed to protect the exploitation of the world's flora and fauna. CITES was originally consigned to monitor and, later, to control totally the importation of orchid species from the wild. Many beautiful species which, a few years earlier, had been common in collections suddenly became extremely rare in cultivation and raising these from seed was not always a viable option. The cost of raising them was high, and as the species sold for far less than the hybrids, demand dropped off. Hybrids reigned supreme.

Orchids today

Toward the end of the nineteenth century, new markets had started to open up; flower corsages were highly fashionable, and cut-flower nurseries were coming to the fore. These firms specialized in orchids whose flowers were popular for wearing, and grew such plants as *Odontoglossum crispum*, cattleyas, and paphiopedilums. As the plants matured and were divided, the stock could be continually increased at no extra cost to the grower, so very large collections of a few selected types were built up in both Europe and the U.S. This led to the eventual mass production of orchid seedlings, which began in the 1920s. As the fashion for wearing flowers diminished, it was replaced by a preference for cut sprays to be used as house decoration. Today this trade is met largely by the Far East, where orchids in their thousands are grown very cheaply in the warm climate and their flowers flown across the world, to arrive in florists' shops within a few hours of being cut. California caters to the whole of North America, while Holland has become the main supplier

Orchids for the home must last a long time in flower and should be easy to care for. Representative of the most popular types available, the orchids illustrated (below) show the rich variety to be found in flower color and shape: from left to right, *Odontoglossum, Cymbidium, Phalaenopsis,* and *Miltoniopsis.*

Doritaenopsis Quevedo (above) is one of the pretty, compact, warm-growing hybrids being raised in California to meet the demand for potted orchids. Like the related *Phalaenopsis*, its consistent flowering over a long period brings it close to being perpetually in bloom.

for Europe and beyond, and Australian-grown flowers are sold all along the Pacific Rim.

The original cut-flower varieties of orchid all differed one from the other, as they were raised from seed. In the first half of the twentieth century, growers would wait years for a plant propagated from a back bulb to grow on to flowering size, and were happy to pay hundreds of dollars for the privilege. However, the advent of meristemming dramatically changed all this. In the 1960s, Professor Morel, at the University of Paris, developed the technique of mass-producing a single clone by extracting a cluster of cells from the center of a new growth and culturing the tissue in the laboratory. The resulting globular mass was continually divided until each piece was allowed to develop into an individual plant, an exact replica of the original. This stunning technique of meristemming has had immediate and far-reaching results, enabling orchids to be raised to order to meet a need and paving the way for numerous laboratories to produce standardized orchids by the millions, to cater to special occasions such as Mother's Day and Easter. The same technique is now helping some third world countries to compete in a global market of cut flowers. The immediate effect was to cause prices to fall, as once-expensive varieties, available to a few, were suddenly being sold in huge quantities.

The stabilizing of varieties has opened up a new potted plant trade for orchids. While the colder climate of northern European countries had made indoor plant growing popular, in Britain the orchid potted plant trade developed directly from the mass production of certain varieties, encouraging sales from garden centers and superstores. Where previously, purchasers had to deal directly with specialist nurseries, they can now buy Dutch-grown orchids from garden centers, as windowsill orchids of a uniform size and shape are produced to bloom for one or two years, to be discarded as soon as they deteriorate. While this is in contrast to the nurseryman's aim of supplying a plant that will continue to grow and bloom for many years in perfect health, it means that busy people can enjoy using orchids to decorate their homes, replacing them as the flowers die. It eliminates the need for maintenance, except for occasional watering, and avoids the responsibility for regular repotting and close attention to the growing regime. In this way, colors can be varied and there is the pleasure of seeing a new orchid bloom in a permanent, but continually changing, display. Everyone can enjoy orchids without having to become an expert unless they wish to.

cool-gr

The vast majority of orchids cultivated today come from among the cool-growing types because their culture is often easier and their heat requirements less. Many growers restrict their collection entirely to cool-growing hybrids without in any way limiting the abundance of variety, such is the huge choice available without having to provide the extra warmth required by intermediate and warm-growing orchids. Cool-growing orchids include those, like cymbidiums and odontoglossums, that live at high altitudes in the wild. Most grow well indoors, provided they are not exposed to excesses of temperature such as may occur in a sunroom, which can easily over-heat in summer, or an area left unheated in winter. Choose a well-lit part of a living room that is not directly in the sun; it should be warm by day and cool at night.

The main genera in this cool-growing section are *Cymbidium*, *Odontoglossum*, *Miltoniopsis*, *Coelogyne*, *Encyclia*, and *Dendrobium*, and those orchids described are among the most popular and the most readily available. Many other orchids that will grow in slightly warmer temperatures for part of the year will be found in the following chapter on intermediate orchids. Unless otherwise stated, orchid species and hybrids can be crossbred only with others in the same genus.

owing

orchids

cymbidiums

It is often said that cymbidiums owe their popularity not to the fact that they are easy to grow, but because they are difficult to kill. When grown well, however, they are among the most rewarding and desirable orchids for growers the world over. One of the loveliest aspects of cymbidiums is their ability to bloom throughout the dull winter months when little else flowers.

Cymbidiums produce leafy, evergreen plants which stand about 60cm (2ft) tall, and over 90cm (3ft) when in bloom. Their hardened pseudobulbs each carry eight long, narrow leaves. The flowers, which may be from 5–10cm (2–4in) across, depending on the type, are carried on a spike that grows from the base of the newest pseudobulb. Flower spikes appear in the latter part of the year, once the summer growing has been completed, and extend throughout the winter until buds become visible and open in their season. Their flowering season now continues almost throughout the year as new hybrids are raised to cover most months.

The flowers, which will last for up to ten weeks, are of an almost waxy texture, the well-rounded sepals and petals of equal size. The lip, which is the third modified petal, is of similar size and kaleidoscopically patterned in a thousand different ways individual to each specific plant. The fantastic color range for cymbidiums extends from pristine white to wholesome pink and red shades, encompassing brown and cream, and also includes spring greens and fresh-faced yellows. Every color except blue can be found in this one genus. Depending on the variety, one flower spike can support from six to fifteen long-lasting blooms, shown at their best when the spike is allowed to arch gracefully and naturally. A large plant that has been grown on to specimen size can provide an astonishing display, with up to six flower spikes in bloom in a single season.

Origins

Cymbidiums have been cultivated for thousands of years, since being revered in ancient China for their sweet fragrance. In Europe, they became known during a period when vast quantities of tropical orchids were being shipped from their native homeland to satisfy the Victorian appetite for all things exotic. *Cymbidium* species originate from northern India, from China across to Japan, and right down through Malaysia and the islands of the Philippines and Borneo, and continuing south as far as northern Australia. The very first

An attractive clone of the popular, fragrant hybrid, Summer Pearl 'Sonya' (left) is a miniature variety. The hybrid comes in a range of colors and extends flowering into the summer months.

The brushed petals and sepals on the lovely Valley Splash 'Awesome' (right) give an unusual bi-colored flower reminiscent of a watercolor in its delicacy. Up to 12 waxy blooms are produced on an upright flower spike taller than the foliage; they will last for 8–10 weeks during the winter. See page 61 for a full entry.

cymbidiums to gain favor in early European collections were the Himalayan species, but the plants proved to be large and cumbersome, and their flowers did not compare with the more exotic and flamboyant cattleyas. Very few of the original *Cymbidium* species are grown now, but a multitude of exquisite hybrids is available which, for the beginner, far outweigh the charms of the wild plants. The species, now mostly rare, can be found in botanical gardens and specialist collections as well as in their natural habitats, where these still exist.

Cultivation

Growing cymbidiums is not difficult, providing a few basic rules are followed, and there is no reason why the plants should not continue to grow for many years. It is quite common to find varieties still existing in established collections raised in the 1920s or 1930s. To understand what a cymbidium requires by way of care, we must look at how the original species grow in the wild. The majority of the species used for hybridizing come from the Himalayas, where the plants grow as epiphytes in the forks of large trees. As old trees die and crash to the ground, the orchids can adapt and reestablish themselves on rocky outcrops or in well-drained soil, where they continue to live for many years. In the high altitude of the mountains, cymbidiums receive dappled sun on bright sunny days with high light levels, while at night there is a considerable drop in temperature, often to below freezing. Because of the elevation, the plants can tolerate low temperatures, which is not always the case in cultivation.

In many parts of the world, such as California, parts of Australia, northern New Zealand, and many African countries, cymbidiums will grow outdoors either as garden plants or under shade houses. But in cooler parts of America and in Europe, the ideal home for cymbidiums is a high-roofed greenhouse or sunroom where they can enjoy plenty of light and fresh air, which imitates their natural conditions. In the spring, you can shade the greenhouse to reduce the heat and prevent scorching the foliage. Leave the shading in place until the end of summer, then remove it to give the plants full light in winter.

Repotting, when necessary, should be carried out in the spring. The potting material (see page 194) needs to be well-draining and durable, and open enough to allow the fast-growing roots to penetrate right through to the bottom of the pot. If you are concerned, about six weeks after repotting, carefully tap one plant out of its pot and inspect the roots. If they remain circling the top, not growing down through the potting material, it is unsuitable and you will have to repot the cymbidium again, using a less dense material. After repotting, keep the plant moist to encourage it to make plenty of new roots.

The pretty color combinations seen in *Cymbidium* Mini Splash 'Fantasy' (right) are the result of breeding programs that go back to the early years of hybridizing at the beginning of the twentieth century.

Many modern green varieties, like Valley Blush, were bred through generations from the scented species, *C. grandiflorum* and retain some fragrance. This winter-flowering clone, Valley Blush 'Magnificent' (left), is an example of the best of Australian hybridizing, which has created a world market for these orchids.

The roots follow the new growth, which continues well into early summer, by which time flower spikes will be showing. These early spring and summer months are critical in initiating the flower spikes.

Once the spikes become visible, they will shoot up like a bullet at the base of the newest pseudobulb until they reach their maximum height. As soon as they appear, insert a thin bamboo cane into the soil close to the spike, but away from the rim of the pot where most of the new roots will be circling; tie the flower spike to the cane as it grows. If left unsupported, the spike may grow out at right angles, making the flowers difficult to display as well as putting them in danger of being accidentally knocked off. You cannot stake unsupported spikes later because the flowers will be badly placed on the stem and will not right themselves once open.

During the latter months of the year in the northern hemisphere, the day length shortens, and light levels drop. Artificial heating will be needed to maintain a healthy temperature, which should drop to not less than 10°C (50°F) at night, rising by a few degrees during the day. Where cloudy weather persists and sunshine becomes a rarity, buds may start to drop; this is the result of an imbalance between the temperature and the amount of light getting to the plants. Keeping the plants too warm at night, as well as the other extreme of being too cold, often combined with dampness, will cause the buds to turn yellow and drop off. This usually occurs when the buds are on the point of opening and chemical changes are taking place within the unopened flower as color pigmentation flows into the petals and sepals.

While little can be done to compensate for lack of sunshine, even filtered sunshine, the daytime temperature can be kept in balance with the humidity to provide the combination of factors that lead to good culture. Artificial lighting is not always a logical option within a greenhouse, but it can be beneficial indoors. Cymbidiums growing well in the greenhouse may be brought indoors for their flowering period, to be enjoyed fully. To prevent the risk of bud-drop, do not disturb the plants until the flowers are all open on the spray.

If you have acquired a *Cymbidium* as a potted plant and wish to grow it on to flower the next year, do not be surprised if the blooms appear in a different season. The plant you purchased or received as a gift may have been reared to

bloom at a specific date, like Christmas or Easter, and the varied and less exact conditions you can provide may well result in a different flowering time. Reflowering will, in any case, only be achieved with patience and attention to detail. If left indoors, where the light is poor compared with outside, and the temperature more or less constant, cymbidiums are unlikely to bloom again and their growth will be soft, with limp foliage. For this reason they do not make good year-round houseplants.

To succeed with cymbidiums, take the plants outside once the last frosts have become heavy dews, and find a shady position. Gradually move them into a more exposed, sunny place until they are sufficiently hardened off to remain where they receive morning or late afternoon sun, but are shaded from the noon sun, which would scorch their leaves. Avoid putting the plants in a north-facing position where the light will be little better than indoors. The base of fruit trees, where dappled sun will reach the plants during the day as the sun passes overhead, would be an ideal position as it most closely resembles a natural habitat. The cooler nights outside, compared with indoors, will encourage tougher growth that is capable of initiating the flower spikes toward the end of summer. As soon as night temperatures begin to drop, bring the plants inside before the danger of a frost becomes a reality.

While cymbidiums are outdoors, pay close attention to their watering needs. Exposed to the sun and wind, they can dry out quickly; but during long rainy spells, they may need to be covered over temporarily with polyethylene sheeting, or moved under shelter to avoid becoming saturated at the roots. Continue to fertilize at every second watering. When you bring your plant back indoors, clean the leaves and remove any dead bracts from around the pseudobulbs. Check it over for insect pests. To make sure none are loitering in the potting material, simply place the plant in a bucket of water for half an hour to purge it of any unwanted visitors. Indoors, find a well-lit position, preferably in a sunroom until the nights become too cold, finally bringing it into a room when the buds have opened once again, where it can remain in all its glory until the first flowers begin to fade. Remove spent flower spikes by cutting them off about 2cm (1in) from the base with a sharp knife or pruning shears. Unless otherwise stated, cymbidiums should be given a position in light shade in summer and full light in winter, reducing their watering in winter. The temperature range is 10°C (50°F) minimum and 30°C (85°F) maximum.

***Cymbidium* Nevada** (left)
Cymbidiums, such as this superb standard yellow hybrid, have been cultivated and hybridized for over one hundred years. This modern variety produces long upright flower spikes in spring, each with a dozen or more blooms. A mature plant can easily carry up to six flower spikes, producing a fantastic display lasting for weeks. The flower spikes first appear in the fall, and as the summer's pseudobulbs mature, they grow steadily throughout the winter. As the stems lengthen, they need support to prevent them from snapping under their own weight. These plants need plenty of headroom and are best suited to cultivation in a greenhouse or sunroom where there is good light all year. If space allows you to grow them indoors, they can spend the summer outside to benefit from the extra light needed to encourage the flowers.

Flower: 10cm (4in) wide
Flower spike: 120cm (48in) long
Plant: 90cm (36in) high
Pot size: 30cm (12in)

***Cymbidium* Maureen Grapes 'Marilyn'** (right)
This fresh, spring green variety has retained all the original hues from the species, *Cymbidium ensiflorum*, which produced the highly acclaimed Peter Pan, a parent of Maureen Grapes. The dense red peppering on the lip is also indicative of the species. The sweet fragrance of the blooms has continued through this special breeding line, developed in New Zealand to fill a gap in the flowering season of cymbidiums. The plant is sequential flowering, with spikes developing at different stages to give a succession of bloom over a long period. Since its first appearance in 1984, this hybrid has been a favorite, unbeatable for its summer flowering.

Flower: 5cm (2in) wide
Flower spike: 90cm (36in) long
Plant: 45cm (18in) high
Pot size: 15cm (6in)

Cymbidium Bruttera (above)

This attractive compact hybrid is among the
first to bloom after the summer growing
season. Free-flowering throughout fall, it
carries a refreshing fragrance to complement
its clear coloring. A medium-sized plant can
yield up to six flower spikes. To ensure a good
crop of flowers, place outdoors for the summer
growing season, which will produce a harder
growth. Once the flower spikes, resembling
fat pencils, are seen at the base of the plant,
bring it indoors into a light position, where it
will flower for weeks.

Flower: 5cm (2in) wide
Flower spike: 90cm (36in) long
Plant: 30cm (12in) high
Pot size: 15cm (6in)

Cymbidium Tangerine Mary (right)

Raised in New Zealand, this latest winter-
flowering hybrid is a breakthrough into the
vibrant colors once seen only in the later,
mid-season varieties. Produced for the home
grower, the plant is compact, with its leaves
held upright, and is less demanding of space
than most cymbidiums. The flower spikes carry
numerous medium-sized flowers, held naturally
upright and reaching no taller than the
foliage. A mature plant will bloom freely
throughout the winter season, producing
flower spikes that open in succession.

Flower: 5cm (2in) wide
Flower spike: 90cm (36in) long
Plant: 60cm (24in) high
Pot size: 15cm (6in)

Hybridizing among cymbidiums continues to improve their color range and their flowering times.

***Cymbidium* Cotil Point AM/RHS** (above)
Cotil Point is an eye-catching hybrid, raised in the Channel Island of Jersey in the late 1990s. It is one of the latest in a long line of superb red-flowered hybrids, giving a wonderful depth of color with quality and substance of flower. It is winning awards on both sides of the Atlantic and has already gained three Awards of Merit from the Royal Horticultural Society in London. The striping on the petals and sepals, often seen in the red-flowered hybrids, expresses the influence of the Indian species *C. tracyanum*, a brown and tan striped flower with a yellow lip. Although used far back in this plant's pedigree, its contribution is clear. The large flowers open in winter and can be left on the plant, or cut singly.

Flower: 15cm (6in) wide
Flower spike:120cm (48in) long
Plant: 100cm (40in) high
Pot size: 20cm (8in)

Cymbidium Cotil Point 'Ridgeway' (left)
Some degree of variation is present with all orchid hybrids, but it is even more noticeable in cymbidiums. Any number of clones from a particular hybrid will show differences in color, shape, and lip markings. There are so many conflicting genes in the makeup of modern hybrids that any one can appear dominant in a flower. Cotil Point 'Ridgeway' shows considerable variation from the clone illustrated on page 59. The similarities are the striped petals and sepals, and the shape of the lip, while the main difference lies in the coloring, which is noticeably lighter in 'Ridgeway.'

Flower: 15cm (6in) wide
Flower spike: 120cm (48in) long
Plant: 100cm (40in) high
Pot size: 20cm (8in)

Cymbidium Bethlehem (above)

This white midwinter-flowering variety can trace its long pedigree back to two white species, *C. eburneum*, a single-flowered plant from India and Myanmar, and *C. erythrostyllum*, a multi- but smaller-flowered species from Vietnam. The influence of the former was to give good shape but few flowers on the early white hybrids. That of the latter, and other breeding plants, helped to overcome this problem to give the long spikes of the modern white hybrids. This Californian-bred hybrid has the slightest blush of pink touching the sepals, while the petals carry a light adornment, highlighted in greater detail on the prettily marked lip. To ensure the plant blooms well the following year, place outdoors for the summer months to produce a strong growth that will ripen well before producing its flower spikes.

Flower:12cm (5in) wide
Flower spike: 120cm (48in) long
Plant: 100cm (40in) high
Pot size: 20cm (8in)

Cymbidium Glowing Valley 'Sunrise' (below)

Behind the majority of all standard hybrids is the most famous cymbidium of all time, Alexanderi 'Westonbirt' FCC/RHS. The influence of this white hybrid, raised in 1922, can still be seen today in the shape and substance of flowers like Glowing Valley, raised in 1985 from the finest Australian stock. This perfectly shaped flower has a hint of shell-pink with a delicately spotted lip, creating a subtle counterpoint to the bolder colorings found in the genus. The very pale-colored flowers can be spoiled by too much bright light and, while they are in bloom, should be kept away from direct sunlight; they will last in perfection for up to ten weeks.

Flower: 9cm (3¹/₂in) wide
Flower spike: 120cm (48in) long
Plant: 100cm (40in) high
Pot size: 20cm (8in)

Cymbidium Valley Splash 'Awesome' (right)

Many of the best *Cymbidium* hybrids are raised in Australia, which has become the breeding center of the world for these orchids. All those with "Valley" in their names are from Valley Orchids in South Australia; Valley Splash appeared in 1991. The brushed petals and sepals on this lovely variety give an unusual bicolored large flower which is slightly cupped. See page 53 for another illustration.

Flower: 10cm (4in) wide
Flower spike: 120cm (48in) long
Plant: 100cm (40in) high
Pot size: 20cm (8in)

**Cymbidium Valley Blush
'Magnificent'** (above)

This is a standard-type *Cymbidium* clone,
capable of producing up to a dozen large,
dramatic flowers per spike, each with spring
green coloring and a delicately spotted lip.
Several spikes appear on a large plant. These
hybrids require good light to initiate the flower
spikes during the late summer but, once the buds
begin to show, they need to be given more
shade. Overexposure to light at this stage can
cause the buds to abort, turning yellow and
dropping off just when you expect them to open.
Once in bloom, keep in the shade to prolong the
flowering and maintain the color.

Flower: 10cm (4in) wide
Flower spike: 120cm (48in) long
Plant: 100cm (40in) high
Pot size: 20cm (8in)

Cymbidium Mini Splash 'Fantasy'
(below)

This hybrid is also bred from the miniature species, *C. pumilum*, but successive crossings with the larger, standard varieties have given a smaller plant with bigger blooms, midway between the two types. The unusual color combination shows a yellow base brushed with red to give the flowers a "tiger" look. The lip markings on Mini Splash, deep yellow spotted with maroon, are reminiscent of the smaller species and create a lovely rich mixture to brighten the dullest of winter days. The long flower spikes need supporting and can be tied to a bamboo cane that is a little shorter than the top of the flower spike; training the spike from an early stage will ensure that it grows upright.

Flower: 9cm (3¹/₂ in) wide
Flower spike: 90cm (36in) long
Plant: 75cm (30in) high
Pot size: 20cm (8in)

Cymbidium Mini Sarah 'Sunburst'
(above)

With a pretty white- and yellow-spotted lip, this is one of a wide range of compact orchids produced to give a shorter plant with smaller flowers, more easily accommodated indoors. Mini Sarah is a direct descendant of the Korean species, *C. pumilum*, a compact-growing, small-flowered orchid. This was overlooked for many years as a potential breeding plant, but from the late 1950s has been used extensively to create the miniature varieties so useful for indoor growing. Several flower spikes can be produced in one season, not all opening at the same time, giving an extended season of bloom. Flowering can carry on through the winter months, well into the spring, during which time the plant needs to be watered and fed regularly to maintain the extra effort required. Repot as soon as possible after flowering. These smaller plants can be left undivided for several years without ever becoming too large to manage easily.

Flower: 9cm (3¹/₂ in) wide
Flower spike: 60cm (24in) long
Plant: 75cm (30in) high
Pot size: 20cm (8in)

the odontoglossum alliance

Odontoglossums and the numerous natural and specially bred genera related to them are highly decorative and easy to grow. Early Victorian growers referred to odontoglossums as the "queen of orchids" because of their petite, dainty blooms which appeared so feminine. Once they had found favor, hybridizing proceeded at a great pace, involving related genera, including *Cochlioda, Miltonia (Miltoniopsis), Oncidium,* and many more, all of which combine to make up the *Odontoglossum* alliance, the resulting man-made hybrids being known as intergenerics. Many species originally classified as odontoglossums have since been botanically separated into genera of their own, and the whole group remains under revision.

Odontoglossums are evergreen plants producing green pseudobulbs and two pairs of flexible, medium-green leaves. The flower spikes come from the base of the leading pseudobulb and may carry from five to literally a hundred or more exquisite long-lasting blooms, produced at almost any time of year. The modern, highly complex hybrids within this extensive group are varied and excitingly different from any other group of orchids. Odontoglossums may be self-colored or patterned and decorated in a multitude of designs. With the exception of green, there is no color not represented, with mauves and purples bordering on blue being predominant, alongside gorgeous reds and yellows, as well as white. This broad spectrum of color is the result of extensive breeding over the last 200 years.

Origins

The original home of most of the *Odontoglossum* types is in the Andes, the huge range of mountains that reaches down through South America. The plants are epiphytic, growing naturally upon forest trees in dappled sunlight, and at high elevations where they are accustomed to cool nights and warm days, with fresh mountain breezes and little seasonal change. The first discoveries were made about 1790, after which these orchids were found right across the Isthmus of Panama, up through Guatemala, and into Mexico. Most of these have now

The individual blooms of this intergeneric hybrid, *Vuylstekeara* Bert White x *Odontocidium* Goldrausen (above), are a deep fiery red. The color extends evenly across the petals and over the lip, with a little white flecking toward the center of the bloom.

ered. *Odontioda* Aviewood (right) illustrates the poetic beauty of a pure white flower, with the occasional dot and central adornment on the lip. See page 69 for a full entry.

been reclassified into other genera, such as *Rossioglossum* and *Lemboglossum*, although the original name remains for the registration of intergeneric hybrids.

To clarify the complex classification of intergeneric hybrids, bear in mind that the names of the first two genera were always amalgamated, so that *Odontoglossum* × *Cochlioda* became *Odontioda*. Where three or more natural genera were crossed together, a new generic name was provided, usually that of the breeder, with the Latin ending -*ara*. Hence, *Odontoglossum* × *Oncidium* × *Cochlioda* gives *Wilsonara*. Today there are dozens of these breeding groups honoring growers and breeders, with thousands of hybrids to choose from. All are members of the *Odontoglossum* alliance and now outnumber the pure *Odontoglossum* hybrids.

Although there exists an abundance of dazzling hybrids to tempt you into growing, few of the species remain in the wild. This is a direct result of mass overcollecting which continued unabated until 1915. While the species are rare and classed as specialist collector's items, the very best *Odontoglossum* hybrids are mass-produced and available worldwide. Their cultivation is the same as for *Miltoniopsis* (see page 82), with watering all year round and a cool, shady position. The only exception is that they can be grown slightly cooler, at a minimum temperature of 10°C (50°F), with a maximum of 24°C (75°F). The ideal pot size, unless otherwise stated, is 10cm (4in).

Odontoglossum bictoniense x Brassia Stardust (left)

Not all the hybrids within the *Odontoglossum* alliance produce the typical well-rounded flowers with wide petals and sepals, and this new hybrid is one of the novelty crosses within this highly variable group. As yet unnamed, it carries the names of its parents for identification. *Brassia* Stardust is a long-petaled, green-flowered type of spider orchid, so-called for its narrow, elongated petals. While the species has provided the long flowering spike with numerous flowers, the Stardust hybrid has increased the size and intensified the color of this charming cross. Breeding from *O. bictoniense* has given rise to some other extremely colorful summer-blooming varieties. These hybrids usually have a resting period in the winter, when they can be kept on the dry side until the new growths are seen.

Flower: 5cm (2in) wide
Flower spike: 45cm (18in) long
Plant: 30cm (12in) high
Pot size: 12cm (5in)
Position: Light shade in summer, full light in winter
Temperature: 10°C (50°F) min., 30°C (86°F) max.

Lemboglossum bictoniense (below)

This Guatemalan species, introduced in 1835, has produced a line of attractive hybrids, particularly with related genera such as *Brassia* (see page 114), but it remains a collectible species in its own right. By using the predominantly pale-lipped *alba*, or darker forms, hybrids in yellow and pink-red can be raised. Flowers, carried on an upright spike, form in two rows along the stem and last a long time. The plant blooms in late summer and forms large clumps within a few years.

Flower: 4cm (1 1/2 in) wide
Flower spike: 45cm (18in) long
Plant: 30cm (12in) high
Watering: Spring, summer, fall; little in winter
Position: Shade in summer, full light in winter

Odontoglossum Geyser Gold

(left)
Raised in New Zealand in 1989 from German parents, this yellow hybrid has been much influenced by its species grandparent, *Lemboglossum bictoniense* var. *alba*, which has given its distinctive light coloring. The pale yellow base is heavily overlaid with deeper yellow blotching, producing a ripple effect of light and dark. The individual blooms are less rounded than many of the modern hybrids, giving a well-defined outline and crisped edges to the petals and sepals. Up to twelve flowers are carried on a long spike, mostly in the fall. This plant is smaller than the typical *Odontoglossum* hybrid and is easy to grow and flower. Darker clones of *Lemboglossum bictoniense* may be used to produce hybrids of similar patterning in pink and mauve colors.

Flower: 5cm (2in) wide
Flower spike: 50cm (20in) long
Plant: 30cm (12in) high
Temperature: 10°C (50°F) min., 24°C (75°F) max.

Odontioda Marie Noel 'Bourgogyne'

(above)
The most highly patterned orchids of all can be found among the *Odontoglossum* hybrids. This modern variety is one of a long line of superb crosses from the long-established, world-renowned orchid nursery of Vacherot & Lecoufle in France. Hybrids like Marie Noel have won numerous awards for outstanding quality and 'Bourgogyne' is one of the finest forms, with its distinctive leopard spotting on the flowers. Their origins, which can be traced back through many generations to the lovely white species, *Odontoglossum crispum*, can still be seen in the crisp, highly ornate white flowers, although they may also be self-colored in almost any shade, except blue or green. The species comes from the Andean mountains of South America where it grows on trees at high altitudes and enjoys cool nights and fresh mountain breezes. The well-rounded blooms, with sepals and petals of equal size, have a small, neat lip which usually carries similar adornment to the rest of the flower.

Flower: 6cm (2 1/2 in) wide
Flower spike: 30cm (12in) long
Plant: 30cm (12in) high

Odontioda Kalkastern (left)

Kalkastern is a recent German-bred hybrid, achieved by using the dark red *Odontioda Feuerkugel* with the species *Lemboglossum rossii* to give a wonderfully colored, compact flower with a broad lip. The blue-mauve color of the lip is greatly sought after in this type of hybrid, and here the rich yellow honey guide clearly shows at the center of the blooms. The advantage of this breeding line is its departure from the more usual rounded, small-lipped flowers, to give a perfectly balanced but overall smaller flower, well-suited to indoor growing. *Lemboglossum rossii* has been successfully crossed with variously colored hybrids, extending the range of colors while retaining the qualities seen here.

Flower: 5cm (2in) wide
Flower spike: 20cm (8in) long
Plant: 30cm (12in) high

Odontioda Aviewood (below)

This British-bred hybrid closely resembles the original species *Odontoglossum crispum*, from which early hybrids were developed in the first half of the twentieth century. The red coloring usually associated with odontiodas (as seen in *O. Kalkastern*, above left) has been completely reversed by the dominance of several generations of *Odontoglossum*, where the flower has gone full circle and, once again, become white. These flowers are produced on long spikes, with up to a dozen per stem, and they can appear at almost any time of the year. Flowers produced during the summer will be of a superior quality to those which come later; those that develop during the winter months, when the light is less intense, will have a pink tinge to the petals and sepals. See also the larger illustration on page 65.

Flower: 8cm (3in) wide
Flower spike: 30cm (12in) long
Plant: 30cm (12in) high

Odontonia Boussole 'Blanche' (left)

Here is a French-bred intergeneric hybrid of exceptional quality, the result of crossing *Miltoniopsis* with *Odontoglossum*. Most odontonias possess the large flamboyant lip of the *Miltoniopsis* parent but, in this instance, the *Odontoglossum* proves to be most dominant. The star-shaped flowers with pointed petals can be traced back to the species *O. crispum*, which has produced all the modern white hybrids. The flared lip and slight pink tinging on the inside of the flower come from its pink-flowered parent, *Miltonia vexillaria*; this coloration is deeper on the outside, as can be seen here in the pink unopened buds. This hybrid has a long pedigree, however, with several other clones contributing through successive generations to the overall excellence of Boussole 'Blanche'.

Flower: 8cm (3in) wide
Flower spike: 30cm (12in) long
Plant: 30cm (12in) high

Odontocidium
Hansueli Isler

(this page)

The brilliant patterning and colorful arrangement of red-brown overlaid on a yellow base is seen even through the buds of this delightful German-bred hybrid. Several modern hybrids are named to honor members of the Swiss Isler family, whose head, Jakob Isler, is a commercial grower. One of Europe's leading hybridizers, he has produced a number of fine modern crosses within the *Odontoglossum* alliance. This plant, with its ornate lip, is very free-flowering, producing sturdy, upright spikes with six to ten blooms on the stem. These are long-lasting but need to be kept out of direct sun or excessive heat while in bloom, as extremes of temperature can cause the fine-looking blooms to wilt prematurely.

Flower: 6cm (2^1/$_2$in) wide
Flower spike: 50cm (20in) long
Plant: 30cm (12in) high

Odontocidium **Purbeck Gold** (below)

This is an older type of British-bred hybrid, first produced in 1983. Still in great demand for its exquisite coloring and large flared lip, it produces a robust plant with tall flower spikes, which blooms mainly in the fall, its yellow and brown coloring perfectly matching the season. The rich yellow is a direct result of using the distinctive Mexican species, *Oncidium tigrinum* as a parent. This strongly textured plant carries the yellow flared lip that characterizes all its progeny. The hybrids also inherit the large pseudobulbs, making them excellent, free-blooming growers, often producing two flower spikes from a single pseudobulb. Regular repotting helps the plant to reach its full potential. Odontocidiums can also be red, red-brown, and red-mauve in coloring, depending on the breeding lines.

Flower: 6cm (2¹/₂ in) wide
Flower spike: 50cm (20in) long
Plant: 30cm (12in) high

Odontocidium **Isler's Goldregen** (above)

The introduction of *Oncidium* adds a further dimension to the *Odontoglossum* alliance. Oncidiums have a predominance of yellow-flowered species, and it is these species (including the much bred-from *O. tigrinum*) which, crossed with yellow odontoglossums, result in some wonderfully rich browns and yellows. Here, the heavy reddish brown overlay almost completely obscures the yellow base color. This large flower has a precise star-shape to the petals and sepals, while the generous lip is flared, a feature gained from *Oncidium*. Some of these hybrids can produce very tall flower spikes which, with their well-sized blooms, are extremely eye-catching. The robust plants produce big pseudobulbs that will bloom at almost any time of year.

Flower: 8cm (3in) wide
Flower spike: 60cm (24in) long
Plant: 30cm (12in) high

Wilsonara Uruapan 'Tyron' AM/RHS (right)

There is as much variation to be found among the wilsonaras as among any of the man-made intergeneric hybrids within the _Odontoglossum_ alliance. _Wilsonara_ is the result of crossing three natural genera, _Cochlioda_, _Odontoglossum_, and _Oncidium_. The first of this trigeneric cross, named after Gurney Wilson, an eminent orchidist, and writer of his day, was flowered in 1916. Very few new wilsonaras were raised until the introduction of _Oncidium tigrinum_ revitalized the genus, creating wonderfully rich combinations, as seen here. They are a fitting testimonial to a man who was awarded the Victoria Medal of Honour by the Royal Horticultural Society in London, for his services to orchidology. This attractive and beautifully symmetrical flower shows the greatest influence of the _Cochlioda_ and _Odontoglossum_ within the breeding. A strong and robust grower, it produces tall flower spikes with up to a dozen blooms on the stem. Its flowering season varies throughout the year.

Flower: 9cm (3^1/$_2$in) wide
Flower spike: 50cm (20in) long
Plant: 25cm (10in) high
Pot size: 15cm (6in)

Wilsonara Kolibri (below)

The *Oncidium* parent has had the greatest influence on this trigeneric hybrid by reducing the flower size but greatly increasing the number of flowers on the spike. These are carried on side branches, giving a pleasing Christmas tree effect. The pink and red coloring of the petals and sepals comes from *Cochlioda*, while the overall shape, although reduced, is typical *Odontoglossum*. This unusual breeding line successfully incorporated the best varieties of the pretty pink and white tall-stemmed species *Oncidium incurvum*, with the smaller, dainty-flowered *Oncidium ornithorynchum* two generations back, showing how different flowers can be produced to create further variety within the *Odontoglossum* alliance.

Flower: 4cm (1¹/₂in) wide
Flower spike: 100cm
 (40in) long
Plant: 18cm (7in) high
Pot size: 15cm (6in)

Wilsonara Widecombe Fair (above)

This captivating pink and white hybrid is the result of using different species within the *Odontoglossum* alliance to give a smaller, more open style of flower. While the plant is typical of the odontoglossums, the flower spike is taller, carrying numerous flowers on side branches. The species, *Oncidium incurvum* has imparted its characteristically long spike and flower shape to the hybrid in a superior form. On the other side of its parentage stands *Odontioda* Florence Stirling, much used in the 1940s and 1950s to endow its progeny with its rich purple coloring. The tall summer-flowering spikes take months to grow and develop their blooms and need supporting from a young age (see page 218). Widecombe Fair is a vigorous hybrid that will grow just as well in a warmer environment of 13°C (55°F) minimum, provided daytime temperatures are kept below 24°C (75°F). This has enabled it to succeed in parts of the U.S. where cool shade is provided.

Flower: 5cm (2in) wide
Flower spike: 90cm (36in) long
Plant: 23cm (9in) high
Temperature: 13°C (55°F) min., 24°C (75°F) max.

Sanderara Rippon Tor 'Burnham' (left)
The trigeneric hybrid, produced by crossing *Brassia*, *Cochlioda*, and *Odontoglossum*, is named after the founder of the famous nursery of Sander & Sons of Saint Albans, England. The first of the genus was registered in 1937. The *Brassia* influence has lengthened and narrowed the sepals and petals to give a more open flower, which is otherwise typical *Odontoglossum* and reminiscent of the earlier hybrids most closely allied to the species. The attractive flowers are produced on a tall, arching stem with up to a dozen large blooms. Their ivory white base color is overlaid with splashes of red and pink on the sepals and petals, intensified at the center of the creamy yellow lip. Its flowering time is various, but it blooms mostly during spring. The plant is tall and robust-growing, its culture the same as for other members of the *Odontoglossum* alliance.

Flower: 8cm (3in) wide
Flower spike: 50cm (20in) long
Plant: 25cm (10in) high
Pot size: 15cm (6in)

Vuylstekeara Linda Isler (above)

Long arching sprays of cheery red and white flowers provide an eye-catching display in this orchid bred by the Swiss Isler family. This hybrid genus contains *Cochlioda, Miltonia,* and *Odontoglossum*: The species that has had the greatest influence is *Miltonia warscrewiczii,* introduced from Peru in 1830. It has followed through two generations, retaining its distinctive open shape. The direct parent of Linda Isler is the outstanding *Odontonia* Debutante 'Oxbow', highly acclaimed in the U.S. and given an Award of Merit by the American Orchid Society in 1960. The flower spikes appear at the end of the growing season when the pseudobulb is complete; once they become long and arching, they need the support of a thin bamboo cane. While flowering, the plant is at rest; new growth starts when flowering is over.

Flower: 5cm (2in) wide
Flower spike: 60cm (24in) long
Plant: 23cm (9in) high

Vuylstekeara Cambria 'Plush' FCC/RHS (right)

This is probably the most popular orchid of all time within the *Odontoglossum* alliance, due to its large, strikingly beautiful, flamboyant flowers, its willingness to bloom, and its ease of growing. The genus is named for Charles Vuylsteke (d.1927), the founder of orchid growing, who established a large commercial nursery in Ghent, Belgium, during the latter part of the nineteenth century. Cambria first appeared in 1931, originating from the famous British nursery of Charlesworth & Co. at Hayward's Heath, Surrey. With the advent of meristem culture, its popularity spread worldwide, and today it can be found in every country where orchids are cultivated. It was awarded its first class certificate in 1967. The plant will bloom twice a year, often producing two flower spikes from one pseudobulb, with up to a dozen long-lasting blooms on each one. Ensure that the pseudobulbs remain in a plump state and are not allowed to get so dry that they become shriveled.

Flower: 8cm (3in) wide
Flower spike: 50cm (20in) long
Plant: 30cm (12in) high

Vuylstekeara Cambria 'Yellow' (below)

Here is the yellow variety of the previous hybrid. Cambria has four instances of the highly variable species *Odontoglossum harryanum* in its early ancestry, and this has influenced the hybrid to the extent that during the mass-cloning process tissue-colored variants were accidentally produced. One of these, 'Yellow', appeared a few years ago in Holland and has since gone on to reproduce true to its color. It is unusual for the technique to throw up a completely different color form, and this freak occurrence has made the plant extremely popular. In all other respects, Cambria 'Yellow' is identical to Cambria 'Plush'.

Flower: 8cm (3in) wide
Flower spike: 50cm (20in) long
Plant: 30cm (12in) high

Rossioglossum grande (above)
The common name for this Guatemalan species is clown orchid, referring to the amazingly life-like shape seen at the center of the flower. This part of the central lip formation entices and guides the pollinating insect to the pollen, hidden behind the anther at the end of the column, here resembling a clown's oversized head. The plant looks like an odontoglossum, to which it is related, although the huge, glossy chestnut and yellow flowers are distinctive and unique in the orchid family. They are produced, several on an arching spike, during the fall, when they last up to three weeks.

Flower: 12cm (5in) wide
Flower spike: 30cm (12in) long
Plant: 30cm (12in) high
Pot size: 15cm (6in)

Cochlioda rosea 'Burnham' (below)
This pretty South American species is a small flower representing a genus closely related to *Odontoglossum*, with which it will readily interbreed to create the man-made generic hybrid, *Odontioda*. (Today there are far more hybrids grown within *Odontioda*.) Both *Cochlioda rosea* and the red-flowered *C. noezliana* have been used extensively to give color to the odontoglossums, originally mainly a white flower. The dainty, self-colored species held much potential for hybridizers and resulted in an explosion of red-flowered odontiodas after the first one, *Odontioda* Vuylstekeae, was registered in 1904. The early crosses were easily recognized by their vivid red coloring but after many generations of intermixing the two natural genera, the boundaries have become merged. This species is challenging to grow and hard to find in nurseries, so it is usually grown by collectors or used by nurserymen to create further original hybrids within the alliance.

Flower: 2cm (1in) wide
Flower spike: 15cm (6in) long
Plant: 15cm (6in) high

Burrageara Stefan Isler (above)
Four popular genera have been combined to produce this richly colored hybrid. The man-made genus, an older addition to the extensive *Odontoglossum* alliance, registered in 1927, has been achieved by breeding with *Cochlioda*, *Miltonia*, *Odontoglossum*, and *Oncidium*, the result an eye-catching creation of reds and light reds. The *Miltonia* has influenced the dramatic lip, while the *Cochlioda* gives the flower its rich coloring. The flower size has been slightly reduced by the *Oncidium*, and the whole plant is compact enough for indoor growing. The blooms, with their vivid red sepals and petals, have a contrasting fiddle-shaped orange lip. Carried on side branches to the main stem, they last for several weeks and can be produced at almost any time of year.

Flower: 6cm (2½in) wide
Flower spike: 60cm (24in) long
Plant 23cm (9in) high
Pot size: 15cm (6in)

oncidiums

This is by far the largest genus of the three from the *Odontoglossum* alliance mentioned here, comprising more species than the miltoniopsis and odontoglossums together. They are also far more varied but, surprisingly, not grown in such large numbers. These epiphytic plants are widely distributed throughout South America, as far as northern Mexico, and down through Florida, and including the various islands of the West Indies.

Extremely variable in their growth, oncidiums display several distinct habits. There are those with green pseudobulbs resembling those of the odontoglossums, but producing lengthy flowering spikes, their flowers small and curiously shaped and the dominating lip well-defined and decorative. There is a prominence of bright, golden yellows and soft shades of brown and tan. Another well-known group are the mule-ear oncidiums, whose stiff, erect leaves are mostly solitary, with diminutive, hardly recognizable pseudobulbs. They produce tall flower spikes with bright sunshine-yellow flowers arranged in a spreading effect at the top of the stem. This group can vary from a few centimeters tall to giants with 30cm (12in) leaves and flower spikes reaching to over a meter (3–4 feet). They will grow under slightly warmer conditions than those with true pseudobulbs and need good light to flower well. Growing best in the sunnier parts of the U.S., including Florida and the Southwest, they appeal mostly to specialists and make poor subjects for beginners.

At the other end of the size scale are the tiny, pseudobulbless oncidiums that produce fanned growths, less than 15cm (6in) high. Their flowers are among the most intricate of the popular orchids, and their delicate patterning and vivid colors far outweigh their diminutive size. Bright combinations of red and yellow can be found alongside pastel shades of pink, with yellow presiding among most other colors. Their native habitat is in the West Indies, and they are best grown in a warm, moist atmosphere where there is ample light all year-round. They have an extremely fine rooting system and often do better attached to pieces of bark than in pots. They are challenging orchids to grow, but will reward with an abundance of flowers.

The finest hybrids among the oncidiums have come from Mexican species such as *O. tigrinum* and *O. incurvum*; these are the pseudobulbous varieties which, when crossed with the Andean odontoglossums, produce the vibrant colors

Oncidium flexuosum

(above & right)

This yellow-flowered Brazilian species introduced in 1821 has blooms that are typical of many in the genus. The narrow petals and sepals, lightly barred with chestnut brown, are quite insignificant compared to the large, exaggerated, deep yellow lip that flares out into a broad, flat surface. Sometimes given the fanciful name of "dancing ladies," the lips resemble the swirling skirts of female figures as the orchids dance in a gentle wind. The small flowers are carried at the end of a long flower spike, on side branches that give an attractive shower effect. The plant produces pseudobulbs at intervals, with a length of rhizome in between, enabling it to gain height, which is ideal for scrambling up a tree branch in its natural environment. In cultivation this makes keeping the plant in a pot hazardous, so it is better grown on a piece of cork bark, or in a pot with a mossy pole inserted. When well-grown, numerous aerial roots are produced, which are an exciting part of the plant. This plant blooms in the fall and lasts several weeks in flower. Water less in winter when it is resting.

Flower: 2cm (1in) wide
Flower spike: 60cm (24in) long
Plant: 20cm (8in) high
Pot size: 12cm (5in)

and finely chiseled flowers of the odontocidiums. They are vigorous, stout plants resembling a large *Odontoglossum*, the flower spikes tall and sometimes branching, and the boldly colored flowers highly varnished in combinations of rich mahogany, or plum, bright yellow, or tiger brown, distinguished by large yellow lips. These intergeneric hybrids are the best of the group to grow. Sturdy, stunningly beautiful, and tolerant of cool to warmer conditions, they are at home indoors, or in a greenhouse, where they can be given good light and plenty of water, with fertilizing throughout the year. In temperate climates, they can spend the summer outdoors, the harder growth produced by this treatment ensuring a breathtaking display of flowers each year.

Cultivation

Oncidiums, like most of the complex hybrids within the *Odontoglossum* alliance grow in a nine- or ten-month cycle. This is the time the plant takes to produce one pseudobulb, after which it blooms and the next seasonal growth starts. Repotting, when necessary, should therefore be done when there is a new growth just showing. By avoiding the coldest and the hottest months of

Oncidium Aloha Iwanaga (left)
The oncidium hybrids have become increasingly popular with the advent of further breeding that has given a much wider variety of color and flower shapes. This yellow-flowered Hawaiian-bred hybrid can trace its ancestry back to three species, _O. flexuosum_, _O. sphacelatum_, and _O. varicosum_, all a delightful yellow, with which it shares similarities of shape and structure, including the flared lip typical of the genus. These species, which originate from South and Central America, are seen less and less in cultivation, but their legacy continues in the sparkling hybrids raised from them. This pretty hybrid produces tall flower spikes with modestly sized blooms on side branches along the stem. The petals and sepals are small and narrow, the yellow base dotted with chestnut brown towards their centers. The large, robust plants are mainly summer-flowering and will grow in warmer temperatures as well as the recommended cooler temperatures.

Flower: 5cm (2in) wide
Flower spike: 100cm (40in) long
Plant: 30cm (12in) high
Pot size: 15cm (6in)

the year, you can repot a plant during spring or fall, provided it is not in flower. Repotting immediately after flowering, before the plant has started to grow, can cause the pseudobulbs to shrivel, so delay it until you see the growth developing well, but before new roots are produced. These fine roots, white with green growing tips, can become extensive within the pot, so the potting material should be open and well-draining; a fine grade of bark chippings suits them well. Plants with tall flower spikes need supporting from the time they emerge to when they are in advanced bud; use a thin cane to hold the spike upright to the base of the buds, when it can be allowed to arch naturally.

Where a minimum winter night temperature of 10°C (50°F) is maintained, most plants within the _Odontoglossum_ alliance can be grown together. Plenty of fresh air, together with cool summer days, are important to these high-altitude orchids. The daytime temperature should not rise above 24°C (75°F), and this can be controlled more easily in the home. Continual damping down and sufficient shading, combined with open ventilators day and night, should be enough to keep the greenhouse cool. In warmer parts of the world, a shade cloth construction that allows fresh air in from all sides is a good idea. For all odontoglossums, think shade! Continue watering all year round and, unless otherwise stated, use a 10cm (4in) pot.

Oncidium ornithorynchum (below)

This pretty species from Mexico and Guatemala is still widely grown today, making its mark among the larger modern hybrids. First described in 1815, it did not come into general cultivation until some years later; a few hybrids have been made from it. The name *ornithorynchum* derives from the Greek and means "beak of a bird," a reference to the replica of a tiny dove's head which can clearly be seen at the center of the bloom. It is notable for its strongly fragrant, rosy pink flowers, which are numerous on the compact flowering spikes, the individual blooms small and beautifully formed. The flowers appear in the fall at the end of the growing season, after which the plant has a brief rest. Similar to an *Odontoglossum*, this plant is smaller in stature but will readily produce more than one pseudobulb in a season. Grow it with other odontoglossums and keep out of direct sun.

Flower: 2cm (1in) wide
Flower spike: 20cm (8in) long
Plant: 20cm (8in) high

Oncidium Sharry Baby 'Sweet Fragrance' (above)

Yellow is the predominant color among the oncidiums, but by no means all are yellow. This lovely Hawaiian-bred hybrid, raised along a different breeding line, has produced flowers that show the deep red coloring associated with cochliodas, accompanied by a strong chocolate fragrance, unusual among oncidiums, making this a popular plant for the amateur grower. The pretty, well-defined lip has the pinched middle and flared base found in *Oncidium ornithorynchum* (see left) on one side of its parentage. The numerous flowers are produced on side branches on the spike, which can be trained upright or allowed to arch naturally.

Flower: 2cm (1in) wide
Flower spike: 60cm (24in) long
Plant: 25cm (10in) high
Pot size: 15cm (6in)

Miltoniopsis Zoro x Saffron Surprise (below) shows a yellow coloring unusual in the genus. It has been painstakingly extracted by careful selective breeding, mainly in the U.S. See page 88 for a full entry.

miltoniopsis

These beautiful "pansy orchids," loved for their huge flat blooms with fanciful pansy faces, were once classified as odontoglossums before being split from them botanically. They are similar in appearance and share similar habitats, which range through the high Andes in Colombia to Peru and Ecuador. The most favored species come from Colombia, producing glistening flowers in shades of pastel pink and white. Those from elsewhere were divided off yet again into the genus *Miltonia*; these lack the large appealing flowers but produce smaller, elegantly refined blooms on longer sprays.

Miltoniopsis have two main flowering seasons, which peak in early summer and again in fall. They are extremely free-flowering, regularly producing two or three flower spikes on one pseudobulb. There can be up to six blooms on a spray, their highlight being the gloriously radiant decoration on the lip known as the mask. This is always in stark contrast to the rest of the flower, where colors sweep through dazzling white, primrose yellow, pretty shell pinks, until the deepest of rich reds emerge, close on purple and mauve. These wondrously colored flowers also carry a sweet honey fragrance which, on a warm sunny day in the greenhouse, fills the air from morning to night. While the odontoglossums have long been prized as cut-flower orchids, *Miltoniopsis* flowers do not last when cut from the plant. Blooms that will remain on the plant for five to six weeks in perfection will droop immediately once they have been cut.

As we have seen, *Miltoniopsis* freely interbreed with other members of the *Odontoglossum* alliance; the most popular of these intergeneric hybrids is *Vuylstekeara*, resulting from the crossing of *Odontioda* (*Odontoglossum* × *Cochlioda*) × *Miltonia* (*Miltoniopsis*). Apart from the highly acclaimed *Vuylstekeara* Cambria (see page 75), there is limited interest in intergeneric breeding and the greatest advance is seen within the miltoniopsis themselves, where new color combinations are forever delightfully changing.

Miltoniopsis St Helier 'Plum' (above) is one of the Jersey-bred orchids whose bold decorative designs include the butterfly-shaped mask at the center of the flower. See page 85 for a full entry.

Miltonia clowesii (right) is a species from Central America belonging to a small genus once included among the odontoglossums, but now separated from it. The plants are related, however, and some interbreeding has given further variety to hybrids within the **Miltonia** genus. See page 91 for a full entry.

Cultivation

Miltoniopsis make superb display orchids for both indoor and greenhouse culture. Their foliage is of a softer texture than that of the odontoglossums and a lighter green. Excessive amounts of light cause them to turn pale and insipid, so an indoor environment is ideal for them. Create a cool, shady area where there is some humidity from a tray of wet pebbles and keep the plants evenly moist at the roots throughout the year. Avoid overwatering but do not allow the pseudobulbs to shrivel from being too dry, otherwise this will cause corrugation of the young leaves. The plants may be lightly fed during the summer months. Their delicate foliage is easily marked and they should not be sprayed overhead; it is better to keep the leaves, and especially the flowers, dry at all times. Never overpot the plants, as this can lead to their being overwatered, so grow them in as small a pot as possible (usually 12cm/5in) and repot annually, or at eighteen-month intervals. *Miltoniopsis* can be "shifted on" into a slightly larger pot for several years without disturbing the existing rootball. Only after a long period of time, when the potting material at the center of the rootball has deteriorated and there are dead roots in the middle, need they be repotted into fresh soil and have their fine, extensive roots thinned out.

While *Miltoniopsis* are regarded as cool-growing orchids, they will exist happily in slightly warmer conditions. Dropping the temperature to the coolest in the range, as is possible with cymbidiums, will not be good for these orchids. Prolonged cold and damp can be detrimental, so it is better to keep them on the slightly warmer, rather than cooler, side, which is why most indoor conditions suit them well. Unless otherwise stated, the ideal temperature range for *Miltoniopsis* is a minimum of 12°C (54°F) and a maximum of 25°C (77°F). Watering should continue all year, and they like to be kept in a growing position away from direct sun.

Miltoniopsis Lyceana 'Stampland' FCC/RHS (below)

This lovely two-colored variety has the large lip typical of the genus, which has become the most attractive part of the flower, especially when the central mask is well-defined and of a contrasting color. It is an older hybrid, raised in Britain in 1925, by the famous odontoglossum specialists, Charlesworth & Co. of Haywards Heath, England. This was a time when hundred of similar crosses were being made, all from a very few species such as *Miltonia vexillaria* and *M. roezlii*, from which came outstanding hybrids like Lyceana. The clone 'Stampland' was awarded its first class certificate in 1926, when it became the benchmark for future generations.

Flower: 10cm (4in) wide
Flower spike: 23cm (9in) long
Plant: 30cm (12in) high

Miltoniopsis vexillaria 'Josephina' (above)

Miltoniopsis vexillaria has had the greatest influence of all on the modern *Miltoniopsis* hybrids; it can be found in the background of almost every variety, having been used extensively through several generations to produce today's showy hybrids. Brought into cultivation in 1872, it had been known of since 1867, when it was described as *Odontoglossum vexillarium* and known as "the scarlet odontoglossum." The species is unique in its soft pastel coloring and its large flat flowers on gently pendent sprays. It blooms in early summer when its fragrant flowers will last up to three weeks. Today this is a collector's plant, prized for its natural beauty and maintained in specialist nurseries where it is still used for breeding. It is no longer wild-collected from its native Colombia for commercial distribution—those plants found in cultivation are propagations of stock plants that are many years old.

Flower: 10cm (4in) wide
Flower spike: 23cm (9in) long
Plant: 30cm (12in) high

Miltoniopsis Saint Helier 'Plum' (right)

This colorful variety of the Jersey-bred Saint Helier orchids illustrates the variation that can occur with the same hybrid, but different individual clones (see also 'Pink Delight', page 86). Raised in 1989, this is one of the very best clones, with the exquisite bold patterning at the center of its flower. When a new hybrid is made, the resulting seedlings will all flower differently, each having its own specific markings, some taking more after one parent than the other. Only the best clones are selected for mass propagation by meristem culture, which makes some of the finest orchids, such as this, available from different outlets across the world.

Flower: 10cm (4in) wide
Flower spike: 23cm (9in) long
Plant: 30cm (12in) high

Miltoniopsis Cindy Kane x Beethoven
(below)

The patterning on this highly individual flower has become subtle on the petals, with striking veining on the sepals. The lip carries the lovely "waterfall" design that has been bred into several of the hybrids and can be traced back through many generations to the species *M. phalaenopsis*, which has a highly patterned teardrop lip. This patterning is much sought after and not always obtainable in such a defined manner as seen here. You could expect to pay more for hybrids with this decoration, which is seen mainly in the pink and red varieties. This new hybrid has not yet been named, so retains the parent names until registered in its own right.

Flower: 10cm (4in) wide
Flower spike: 23cm (9in) long
Plant: 30cm (12in) high

Miltoniopsis Saint Helier
'Pink Delight' (above)

This charming clone of Saint Helier is another example of the variation to be found in the Jersey-raised hybrids. It produces high-quality, long-lasting blooms at their best in spring, offering a combination of light, veined pink on the lip, dominated by the dark red butterfly-shaped mask at the center; a broad white border separates the colors. This beautifully balanced flower was raised in Jersey by the Eric Young Orchid Foundation, among the world leaders in hybridizing this genus since the 1970s.

Flower: 10cm (4in) wide
Flower spike: 23cm (9in) long
Plant: 30cm (12in) high

Miltoniopsis **Mrs J B Crum 'Chelsea' FCC/RHS** (this page)

There are many fine red hybrids available, but few illustrate the richness of this outstanding variety. The flower's velvety appearance is enhanced by the white margin around the lip. This is an older hybrid raised in 1931 and bred from Lyceana 'Stampland' (see page 84); it received its first class certificate the following year. Water can spoil the blooms, so take care when watering. Flowers produced in the main spring flowering season will be of a superior quality to those produced later in the fall, though a second flowering is always welcome.

Flower: 10cm (4in) wide
Flower spike: 23cm (9in) long
Plant: 30cm (12in) high

Miltoniopsis Zoro x Saffron Surprise

(right)

In this fine yellow flower of exceptional quality, a deep red brown mask is combined with the two "thumbprints" on the petals, enhancing the bloom and creating a further color dimension. The yellow hybrids are extremely difficult to produce because yellow is not a prominent color found among the species, and many will tone down to cream shortly after opening. By careful selective breeding, done mostly in the U.S., using yellow-tinted forms of M. *vexillaria*, the hidden color has been painstakingly extracted and will continue to be improved upon. Allow orchids like this to grow on to become specimen-sized, without dividing, for a number of years. A large plant with several new pseudobulbs flowering at once will give an impressive display and extend the period of bloom, as not all the flowers will open at the same time.

Flower: 10cm (4in) wide
Flower spike: 23cm (9in) long
Plant: 30cm (12in) high

Miltoniopsis **Eureka** (below)

This lovely, clear yellow variety points the way to a differently colored range of hybrids, vying for attention with the rich reds and pinks. An outstanding variety with soft buttery tones, Eureka is an American hybrid raised in 1980, one of the latest in a successful line producing the elusive yellow coloring. Behind it lies Emotion, a salmon pink hybrid which can be traced back to *M. vexillaria*; it produced one of the most notable yellows, the French-bred Alexander Dumas, which is in fact the parent of Eureka. With twice-yearly blooms from a modest-sized plant, it is an ideal first orchid, offering good rewards for a minimum of care. When in bloom, keep the flowers out of strong light to ensure they last as long as possible.

Flower: 10cm (4in) wide
Flower spike: 23cm (9in) long
Plant: 30cm (12in) high

Miltoniopsis **Robert Strauss** **'White Flag'** (above)

Only a few of the top-quality hybrids have flowers of the purest white, as illustrated in this excellent clone in which the central markings of red and yellow set off the flower. Several clones of Robert Strauss have won awards, a testimony to the consistently high quality of this hybrid, raised in Britain in 1980. The outstanding quality of this variety is the roundness of its flamboyant lip, which is in perfect balance with the size of the petals and sepals. The adult plant carries four to six large blooms on a spike, and it is normal for a well-grown plant to produce two flower spikes from each side of the pseudobulb at the same time.

Flower: 10cm (4in) wide
Flower spike: 23cm (9in) long
Plant: 30cm (12in) high

Miltonia spectabilis (left)

Closely related to the colorful *Miltoniopsis* are the miltonias. The flowers are generally smaller and less flamboyant, although the resemblance is clearly seen in the dominant lip with attractive markings. One of the main differences, seen in this species introduced from Brazil in 1837, is that the miltonias produce a single bloom on a stem and lack the fragrance of *Miltoniopsis*. In fact, the miltoniopsis were once classified with the miltonias and all were known as miltonias, as they still are for hybrid registration purposes. The botanical split separated the Colombian *Miltoniopsis* from the Brazilian *Miltonia* to create two distinct genera. Although closely related, these two genera will not breed together, which is surprising considering that *Miltoniopsis* will cross readily with other related genera, such as *Odontoglossum*.

Flower: 10cm (4in) wide
Flower spike: 10cm (4in) long
Plant: 15cm (6in) high

Miltonia clowesii (left)

This species has typical star-shaped flowers, with erect and pointed lateral petals and fiddle-shaped lip; spaced well apart on a tall, upright spike, they are richly colored, waxy, and fragrant. The main flowering season is summer and fall. Cultivated since 1839, it was discovered near Rio de Janeiro and sent to the Rev. John Clowes of Manchester, after whom it is named. The plant produces modest pseudobulbs with slender leaves, similar to an *Odontoglossum*. See also page 83.

Flower: 5cm (2in) wide
Flower spike: 60cm (24in) long
Plant: 30cm (12in) high
Pot size: 15cm (6in)

Miltoniopsis Nancy Binks (above)

The lip of this lovely variety shows an outstanding pattern, resembling a velvet cushion, at the center of the flower, while the cherry red on the petals contrasts with the white background. This is a recent hybrid, registered in 1985 and raised by an amateur grower, Dr. Jim Binks—proof that the hobbyist can sometimes produce a hybrid to equal the successes of commercial nurseries. Allow the flower spikes to assume their natural arching habit, in order to show off the blooms.

Flower: 10cm (4in) wide
Flower spike: 23cm (9in) long
Plant: 30cm (12in) high

coelogynes and encyclias

Coelogyne ochracea (above) is one of the prettiest species. In spring the flower spike carries up to a dozen sparkling white fragrant flowers, their lips attractively patterned in orange, yellow, and brown.

These charming orchids make ideal indoor plants, since they quickly adjust to the drier atmosphere, produce a long-lasting flowering display, and have a superb fragrance. The two distinct genera are grouped together horticulturally because their cultural requirements are identical, and in their growth, they exhibit similarities of size and adaptability.

All coelogynes and encyclias are compact, evergreen plants, with a fine rooting system, mostly grown in pots. Their pseudobulbs may be rounded, oval, or, as in some encyclias, long and thin. They produce a pair of leaves from the top of the pseudobulb where, with a few exceptions, the flower spike emerges. Among coelogynes, the pseudobulbs are often crowded, growing close together and clump-forming on a large plant. Flowering extends from early spring to late summer; their flowers are enchanting, often sweetly fragrant and long-lasting. Coloring is predominantly white or creamy white, with yellow, light brown, green, and orange-red also represented. Some encyclias hold their flowers with the lip at the top, all coelogynes with the lip at the bottom.

There are very few hybrids available within these two genera, and it is the species, which propagate freely, that are grown. Many have been in cultivation from the time of their original importation over 100 years ago. The cool-growing coelogynes range from China down to India, and as far south as New Guinea, including many of the islands that exist between the two mainlands. Others from Malaysia grow under warmer conditions, and are covered in the next chapter. The encyclias are from the New World, covering parts of South America but mostly found in Mexico and the West Indies; all are cool growing.

Cultivation

Both coelogynes and encyclias have a resting period of several weeks during

winter, before any new growth is seen in spring. The signal to start watering again is once the new growth extends from the base. In most coelogynes, the flower spike develops early from within the center of the young growth, to produce spring blooms. Encyclias complete most of their growing before the flower spike emerges from between the top leaves, in early summer. During this time, water the plants well, keeping them evenly moist at the roots, and giving light applications of fertilizer every second or third watering. Once they start to grow,

Encyclia Sunburst (left) is an ideal windowsill plant that retains its compact stature and easy flowering. It blooms in summer as the pseudobulbs mature and needs a rest in winter. See page 96 for a full entry.

Coelogyne barbata (below)
This tall Indian species became popular after about 1878 when the first living orchid plants were sent from the Khasi Hills. It produces egg-shaped pseudobulbs topped by a pair of dark green, narrow oval leaves; the flower spikes appear between the leaves as the pseudobulb develops. Once this has matured, the buds advance, and the plant blooms in winter. The large flowers are white with a dark brown bearded lip and a fringe of black hairs around the margin. The blooms open in succession along the stem. No longer wild-collected for export, in cultivation this *Coelogyne* grows well from propagations.

Flower: 5cm (2in) wide
Plant: 30cm (12in) high
Pot size: 10cm (4in)

coelogynes often shrivel as the new growths take their nourishment from the older pseudobulbs before the new roots develop; but within a short time, the pseudobulbs fill out again. Overhead spraying is also beneficial during growth.

Keep the plants well shaded during the summer, gradually extending the amount of brightness until they are in full light for the winter. At the start of the inactive period, the plants should be supporting well-matured, plump pseudobulbs storing enough water to take them through the dry rest. Only water them in winter if some shriveling starts; alternatively, spray the leaves to prevent dehydration.

A bark potting mixture will suit these orchids, and, while they can be grown in pots, they can also be accommodated in hanging baskets and left to grow to specimen size if there is room. Where space is limited, keep them small by dividing every three years. Unless otherwise stated, provide a minimum temperature of 10°C (50°F) and a maximum of 30°C (85°F).

Coelogyne mooreana 'Brockhurst' FCC/RHS (right)

This species, discovered in Vietnam as late as 1906, was named after F.W. Moore of the Glasnevin Botanic Gardens in Dublin, Ireland. One of the biggest species in the genus, it produces spectacular, large, pristine white blooms with broad sepals and petals, and a similar shaped lip, which carries a deep yellow stain at the center. The variety 'Brockhurst', a superior form of the species, received its first class certificate the same year. The handsome plant has cone-shaped pseudobulbs with a pair of light green, narrowly oval leaves; do not let the bulbs shrivel. The strong, robust grower is equally at home in a greenhouse or light area indoors.

Flower: 9cm (3½in) wide
Plant: 45cm (18in) high
Pot size: 18cm (7in)

Coelogyne Memoria William Micholitz 'Burnham' AM/RHS (left)

This wonderfully colored hybrid with its glistening white petals and sepals and lip of almost solid gold is an outstanding cross in a genus that has produced very few hybrids of note. The plant has been raised from C. mooreana and C. lawrenceana and was named in honor of the German discoverer of both species, William Micholitz, a nineteenth-century plant hunter who introduced many new plants, including orchids, to the western world. This hybrid produces a large plant with robust, cone-shaped pseudobulbs and a pair of medium green oval leaves. It blooms during spring and early summer, on a flower spike carrying up to six blooms.

Flower: 9cm (3½in) wide
Plant: 45cm (18in) high
Pot size: 18cm (7in)

Coelogyne fuscescens (below)
At the smaller end of the scale, this pretty dwarf-flowering *Coelogyne* species is an ideal windowsill orchid that will never outgrow its position. A native of India and Nepal, it was first described in 1830. The oval-shaped pseudobulbs carry two leaves, from between which the single flower is produced, buff brown with a prettily marked lip. A large plant will be covered with blooms in the fall. The plant will divide readily into smaller pieces if space is limited or, when allowed to grow on, it will form a dense mat of growths to cover its container. There are several similar small species such as this one, and a group growing together makes an interesting feature.

Flower: 4cm (1 1/2 in) wide
Plant: 30cm (12in) high
Pot size: 5cm (2in)

Encyclia Sunburst (left)

This is one of only a very few hybrids that have been raised from the brightly colored species, *Encyclia vitellina* (shown below), the other parent being the highly fragrant *E. radiata* (see page 99). The resulting cross, first raised by E. Iwanaga of Hawaii in 1962,

Encyclia vitellina (below)

Unusual among the encyclias is this species unique in the genus for its bright, vermilion red flowers. The sepals and petals are oval and equally presented and the small duckbill-shaped lip is orange. The flower spike is usually held upright above the plant and carries up to a dozen flowers, blooming in late summer and fall. The plant originates from Mexico and was first described in 1833.

It remains popular among enthusiasts, though very little hybridizing has been done with this species, and the few hybrids raised have not retained the vivid coloring that makes it so highly desirable.

Flower: 2cm (1in) wide
Plant: 15cm (6in) high
Pot size: 8cm (3in)

has given a plant with flowers that are midway between the two parents. Long-lasting and produced on an upright flower spike, they open a delicate shade of apricot and tone as they mature to creamy white.

Flower: 3cm (1 1/4 in) wide
Plant 15cm (6in) high
Pot size: 10cm (4in)

Encyclia brassavolae (right)

Among the encyclias is a group that carries spindly flowers on a flower spike from the apex of the elongated pseudobulb, one of the most colorful of which is *E. brassavolae*. The upright spike carries up to a dozen light green flowers, the oval-shaped lip being white, with the end tipped rosy mauve. This plant blooms during the summer months, when the flowers will last for a long time. The species has tall, slender pseudobulbs with two narrowly oval leaves and originates from Central America, where it grows at high altitudes. In a pot, the pseudobulbs may be well spread out and will quickly fill the surface space; it is better grown in a hanging wooden slatted basket, which gives extra surface area with less potting material underneath. Orchids growing in hanging baskets are more suited to greenhouse or sunroom culture.

Flower: 4cm (1 1/2 in) wide
Plant: 30cm (12in) high
Pot size: 15cm (6in)

Encyclia alatum (below)

This species comes mainly from Mexico and Honduras and is a low-altitude plant found at up to 100m (33ft) in forested areas. One of a group distinguished by their hard cone-shaped pseudobulbs, it has long, leathery leaves, which may be two or three to a pseudobulb. The long flower spike bears from a few to many flowers; though these are quite variable, the yellowish green petals and sepals are usually equal in size, and the decorative lip off white, with some purple lines at the center. The flowers are slightly fragrant and bloom between spring and fall, requiring good light to flower well.

Flower: 2cm (1in) wide
Flower spike: 30cm (12in) long
Plant: 18cm (7in) high
Pot size: 12cm (5in)

Encyclia lancifolia (below)

This pretty, highly fragrant Mexican species is one of several that have similar creamy white flowers with a cockleshell-shaped lip held at the top. The long sepals and petals hang loosely below the lip in a manner slightly reminiscent of the fully expanded fruiting body of an earth star fungus, found in winter in European woods and sandy places. The compact plant has short, club-shaped pseudo-bulbs and a pair of light green leaves; the upright flower spike comes from between the leaves. This is an ideal species for the indoor home grower looking for compact plants with interesting flowers that will not take up too much room; it grows and flowers with great ease and is happy with minimal care.

Flower: 2cm (1in) wide
Flower spike: 15cm (6in) long
Plant: 18cm (7in) high
Pot size: 12cm (5in)

Encyclia cochleata (below)

A large number of encyclias produce their flowers with the lip at the top, in a position we would regard as upside down. *Encyclia cochleata* is known as the cockleshell orchid, a reference to its shell-like lip, and also as the octopus orchid, alluding to its long, drooping, ribbonlike petals. It was the first tropical epiphytic orchid to bloom in Britain, which it did at the Royal Botanic Gardens in Kew in 1763. Green and black flowers come from the top of the club-shaped pseudobulb in a succession lasting weeks or months, depending on plant size. A wonderful orchid for the beginner, it starts flower-ing on a very young plant, then gives unlimited exotic-looking flowers; once it reaches maturity, it becomes perpetually blooming.

Flower: 3cm (1¹/₄in) wide
Flower spike: 15cm (6in)
Plant: 30cm (12in) high
Pot size:12cm (5in)

Encyclia radiata (above)

This is another delightful encyclia to grow. The plant produces slender pseudobulbs with a pair of medium green leaves; the upright flower spike comes from the top of the pseudobulb and carries up to a dozen cheerful little blooms. These have a strong fragrance, and on a large plant, the scent will fill a room. Found in Guatemala, Honduras, and Mexico, this plant is easily grown on to become specimen size as it rarely drops its foliage and will remain looking good for many years without needing to be divided (unless this is to increase the number of plants). The plant blooms during the summer months and lasts for a long time in flower.

Flower: 2cm (1in) wide
Flower spike: 15cm (6in)
Plant: 18cm (7in) high

dendrobiums

Prima Donna (left) is a *Dendrobium nobile*-type hybrid with regal blooms. The Indian species has had a dramatic effect on the flowers raised from it, well-rounded in shape and heightened in coloring.

Dendrobiums are an immense genus, with hundreds of species. Their extremely wide geographic distribution extends throughout Asia, as far north as China, and through the whole of the mainland down to the islands of the Philippines, Borneo, and New Guinea, as well as most parts of Australia and New Zealand's North Island. With such a vast distribution, there have evolved many distinct types, some of which have become very popular with enthusiasts and have produced many colorful hybrids. Others, more obscure, are of less general interest, but all are rewarding to grow. These successful plants have adapted to almost every climate, occupying precarious positions on trees as epiphytes, clinging to rocks as lithophytes, and embedded in narrow crevices. They are found in high-altitude mountain habitats and lower down in the hot, steamy jungles to sea level, even in the dry, arid desert conditions of parts of Australia.

Dendrobium nobile types

Dendrobium nobile is a pretty species originating from the Himalayas, which has been in great demand for over a hundred years. Today it has been superseded by a multitude of superior hybrids, available in a bewildering array of colors, produced by crossing *D. nobile* with related species to bring together the finest qualities of each. The pioneers in the breeding of this greatly enhanced group, known collectively as *Dendrobium nobile*-type hybrids, have been the Japanese growers, whose expertise has created their wonderful color combinations.

These plants produce tall, jointed pseudobulbs, loosely termed canes, giving rise to their common name of "bamboo orchids." The pseudobulbs can grow to 30cm (12in) or more tall, with short, oval, flexible leaves in alternate pairs along their length. Flower nodes are produced from the side of the canes opposite the base of each leaf and develop short stems, each with usually two flowers. These highly decorative flowers are characteristically rounded, with the sepals and petals equal in size, cupped around the circular lip. The colors graduate from whites and yellows to pinks and mauves, the flowers often tipped with brighter shades towards the edge and enhanced by an eye-catching disk at the center. Crimped edges give the flowers an attractive frilly look.

This group of dendrobiums has a fast summer growing period, followed by an extended winter rest. Their cultivation is quite challenging, but the

Dendrobium senile (below) is a pretty dwarf species, only 10cm (4in) high, from Thailand. The elongated pseudobulbs are covered in dense white hairs, forming a protective layer. The waxy flowers, produced in ones and twos on a short stem from the leaf axils, are fragrant and last over several weeks during the spring months. This species has bright yellow flowers with a green center to the lip, their shape typical of many dendrobiums from India and the Far East. The leaves are usually shed after one or two years, and the plant can become completely leafless during the winter rest, when it needs to be in full light and kept dry.

rewards are great because the decorative flowers can cover the entire plant for weeks in spring. Early in the year, these orchids start their new growths from the base of the main plant, as the embryo buds along the canes become active in response to the lengthening days and warmer temperatures. They need little water until the buds are more developed, but from then on, step up watering and add fertilizer to every other watering, so the plants never dry out, until the end of the growing season. New growths develop quickly, followed by an abundance of new roots, while the buds progress fast and the flowers open together along the canes. The flowering canes are usually those of the previous year, although older canes can produce flowers from previously undeveloped nodes. After flowering, place the plants in good light, but not direct sun, for the summer. In warm climates they may spend the summer outdoors in the same way as cymbidiums, giving more light and air to produce a harder growth, which will bloom all the better in spring. Plants grown in a greenhouse should remain where they are, as they will benefit from the relatively high summer daytime temperatures of up to 30°C (86°F). Balance the humidity and spray the leaves regularly, keeping plants moist at the roots.

These fast-growing orchids will complete their season's growth within five months, whereas other orchids may take up to twice as long. By summer's end the long canes will have matured, a single terminal leaf signaling their completion. Yellowish canes indicate that enough light has reached the plants to ripen them prior to winter. From now on, keep in full light and reduce water and fertilizer until, by the end of the year, the plants are dry. They can rest in this state until new activity heralds the start of the growing season, during which the pseudobulbs should remain plump—any shriveling indicates they are not getting enough water, but a good soak in a bucket of water for an hour should put this right. Shriveling during the winter rest may indicate inadequate watering the previous summer, but if too much water has to be given during the winter, the plant will not produce flowers. And if watering is started too early in spring, before the buds are definable, the nodes will become adventitious growths instead of flowers. This natural propagation will provide extra plants in time, but is no compensation for eagerly anticipated flowers. In winter, temperatures with a night-time minimum of 10°C (50°F) are sufficient. Place the plants on a high shelf, close to the glass to get as much natural light as possible.

Tall-growing *D. nobile* hybrids may need support during their growth period or they can become top-heavy and the plant could be damaged by falling over. The plants need to be grown in as small a pot as possible (12cm/5in); they are sometimes overpotted to stop them from becoming top-heavy,

Dendrobium Tancho Queen (left) is a D. nobile hybrid producing the typical canes, jointed along their length. This group flowers on the younger canes while still in leaf. One of the lighter colored hybrids, the beautifully rounded blooms of Tancho Queen contrasts clear white petals and sepals with an almost black disk in the middle of the large frilled lip.

but this can lead to overwatering, which may result in root loss and shriveled pseudobulbs, which then cannot take up water. Where a plant has become top-heavy, place the pot into a larger, heavier container.

Take care when repotting these orchids. It is a common fault to bury the base of the plant too deeply within the potting material, so that the new growth starting from the base is submerged and rots before it has a chance to develop. Always make sure the base of the plant is sitting on top of the soil, not buried beneath it. After repotting, tie the plant to a cane for support until the new roots anchor it firmly. Repot right after flowering; these dendrobiums are not usually suitable for dividing and are better kept intact and shifted on where necessary into a slightly larger pot each time. The old, leafless canes can be used for propagating (see page 212) and the new plantlets grown on to flowering size within a few years. These orchids are semideciduous in cultivation and tend to lose the leaves from one mature cane all at once. This dramatic leaf loss, which occurs at the start of the resting period, is quite natural.

Other varieties

There is a smaller, but no less charming, group of dendrobiums known as the hirsute varieties because of their black-haired pseudobulbs. The best of this type is a widely grown species, *Dendrobium infundibulum*, whose canes are tall and slender and the leaves dark green; flower nodes come from the upper half of the canes in spring. The plant is a native of India, Myanmar, and Thailand and grows happily alongside *D. nobile* types, requiring the same treatment summer and winter. Its large, showy flowers can be 8cm (3in) across the petals, which are pristine white, soft, and papery, with a deep yellow center to the flared lip. These varieties need less light, so are well suited to indoor culture.

In addition, there are many more varied types of dendrobium from the Indian continent, whose flowers are as different from each other as are the plants. They are easily recognized by their typically tall canes, which in some species can exceed a meter (3 feet), and all require similar conditions, with as much variation in temperature between the summer growing season and the winter rest period as possible. While Indian dendrobiums were once plentiful and represented in most collections, today they are found less and less as importing restrictions have led to their decline in cultivation. Since many do not grow easily from seed, they cannot compete alongside the more easily raised *D. nobile* hybrids. Further hybridizing has been successful with native Australian species, and these have produced some gems which, being warmer growing, are discussed in the following chapter.

The distinct *Dendrobium* species and hybrids shown here suggest the huge variation in appearance and characteristics between members of this genus.

Dendrobium infundibulum (above)
This beautiful species, introduced from Burma (now Myanmar) in 1859, produces a handsome plant with tall canes densely covered in fine black hairs. The buds, which emerge in early spring at the start of the plant's growing season, are also protected by black-haired bracts. The flowers appear in threes or fours on stems opposite each leaf axil along the whole length of the cane, each large bloom a delicate papery white with a golden yellow highlight at the center of the lip. This species varies in shape from well-rounded flowers to the more spread-out bloom seen here. This is one of the easiest dendrobiums to grow and flower to perfection, provided it is given plenty of water and light, and moist conditions in the summer growing months.

Although the newest pseudobulbs (canes) produce the flowers, older ones will often give a secondary blooming from nodes at the tip of already-flowered canes. Species from this group will not breed with *D. nobile* types.

Flower: 10cm (4in) wide
Plant: 45cm (18in) high
Pot size: 12cm (5in)

Dendrobium Superstar Champion
(above)

This highly decorative flower is a modern-day *D. nobile* type of hybrid. The plants are a manageable size as their pseudobulbs, or canes, are stout and shortened rather than being long and thin as they are in most of the species. The plants grow well during the summer growing season, making up their canes in a few months. They rest in winter, when they need little or no watering; water only if the pseudobulbs shrivel. The spring will be welcomed by an explosion of buds along the length of the newest pseudobulb, and the flowers will entirely cover the plant. Colors can vary from white, through yellow and pink, to the deeper shades of red-mauve, with contrasting lip decorations.

Flower: 6cm (2¹/₂ in) wide
Plant: 45cm (18in) high

Dendrobium Lucky Seven (below)

Another delightful *D. nobile*-type hybrid, this orchid illustrates the depth of color that can be achieved by selective breeding to bring out its potential richness. The center of the lip is enlivened with an almost black disk which attracts the pollinating insect. These lovely flowers, produced in the spring, have a fuller shape, with more rounded petals and sepals than is apparent in the species; their size has also been increased with selective breeding over several generations. Although bred from species that include some which are deciduous, the hybrids tend to remain evergreen, shedding only a few leaves at a time from the older canes, which then assume a supporting role to the rest of the plant. The older, flowered, and leafless canes can be used for propagating by severing them from the main plant, cutting them into pieces with a node in the center and repotting them in a community pot (see page 212).

Flower: 6cm (2¹/₂ in) wide
Plant: 45cm (18in) high

Dendrobium Oriental Paradise (above)
The group of hybrids on these pages have all
been raised from the species *Dendrobium
nobile* and are often referred to as *D. nobile*-
type hybrids. They exhibit the large, rounded
flowers with a circular lip of equal proportions.
The range of colors among pink, mauve,
yellow, and white shades is almost endless,
each hybrid possessing its own unique lip
coloration and central highlight. Because of
the infinite variations in color, it is best to look
for these plants in flower in the spring to
ensure you select the coloring you like best.
With so many to choose from, a sizable
collection can be made from just this type of
Dendrobium hybrid alone.

Flower: 6cm (2^1/$_2$in) wide
Plant: 45cm (18in) high

Dendrobium nobile var. cooksonii
(below)
In this colorful variety of *D. nobile*, the flower
exhibits the rose-pink coloring of the type,
but also carries a replica pattern of the lip
marking on the lateral petals. Uncommon but
not unknown in orchids, this is called peloria
and can take several forms, such as the lip
repeating the appearance of the petals and
being devoid of any other adornment. In
some instances, this attractive mutation is
encouraged to breed into further generations,
with limited success. This horticultural variant
appeared among a consignment of *D. nobile*
and was grown in the collection of Norman
C. Cookson, a noted grower who exhibited it
for the first time around
1885. All plants now in
cultivation are in fact
propagations of this one
clone. This dendrobium
is capable of flowering
the entire length of its
newest pseudobulbs,
but flowering to such
perfection takes skill.
During the winter the
plant needs a dry rest;
if watering is started too
early in the year, before
the flower buds are fully
developed, they will turn
into adventitious
growths instead.

Flower: 5cm (2in) wide
Plant: 45cm (18in) high

Dendrobium nobile var. virginale

(above)

This pure white Indian species is an all-time favorite that has been in cultivation for almost 200 years. Today it is less popular because it has been·superseded by several generations of superbly colorful hybrids, mostly raised in Japan and Florida. The species produces tall leafy canes which become deciduous after two to three years. Their flowers are carried on short stems in ones and twos along the length of the newest canes, the buds emerging from the nodes that appear along the jointed cane. A number of distinct varieties have occurred naturally within this species, one of which is this lovely albino form, which lacks the usual rose-pink coloring of the type. Adult plants need to have their long pseudobulbs supported with a bamboo cane; to prevent them from becoming top-heavy, place their pots into another larger pot with stones at the bottom. This plant blooms in the spring and will last for three weeks.

Flower 5cm (2in) wide
Plant: 45cm (18in) high

pleiones

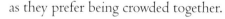

This small genus of extremely popular, modest-growing deciduous orchids come from China, the Himalayan regions of India, as well as from Taiwan and Japan. The plants are mainly terrestrial, growing on moss-covered rocky outcrops and around the base of trees. They develop small, squat, or cone-shaped pseudobulbs with a single leaf, shed in winter. The short-lived pseudobulbs become exhausted after one season and die naturally. Each new pseudobulb will produce several more every year, greatly increasing their number in a short time. These are usually grown together in a shallow pan and give a glorious show of flowers in early spring. The flower spikes come from inside the new growth while it is very young, the thin stems supporting a single flower, rarely two, that are large for the size of plant, at 5–8cm (2–3in) across. The usual colors are pink and white, occasionally yellow, but hybridizing within the genus has improved the color range, the enriched pinks and mauves now vying for attention alongside pure white and apricot shades. While the sepals and petals are long and narrow, the lip is large and flared, fringed at its edge and attractively marked with darker colors.

Because of the ease with which these little plants grow, they are widely available from garden centers selling houseplants, where they are sold as dormant bulbs ready for potting. Grow pleiones in a soilless potting mixture made of equal parts of horticultural foam and coarse sand or grit, with a little horticultural charcoal added. Repot annually immediately after the new growth is seen and before flowering, cutting off the oldest, dead pseudobulbs and the dead roots, leaving just enough to hold the new pseudobulbs and growth firmly in the pan. The new roots will soon be seen just starting at the base of the new growth. Do not bury the pseudobulbs completely in the potting mixture but allow them to settle on the surface. Place as many as you like in a shallow pan, as they prefer being crowded together.

After repotting, water carefully through a rose, but stop the water from getting into the funnel made by the new leaves. Keep the plants evenly watered all through summer, fertilizing lightly at every third watering, and mist the foliage on sunny days. As fall becomes winter, the leaves will turn yellow and drop. Collect fallen leaves together with any surplus bulbils that have formed on the top of the mature

Pleione Versailles (left) is one of many attractive spring-flowering hybrids in this genus. The narrow, oval petals and sepals have a soft, glistening texture and the lip is large, frilled, and delicately colored at the center, with streaks or spotting of a different color.

Pleione speciosa (above)

This species, in cultivation since 1914, is undoubtedly one of the richest-colored in this much-loved genus of small plants. The flowers are typically bright magenta, although intensity of color can vary. Originally just one clone of the species was known, but more plants were later obtained from its native China. The plant has proved to be extremely good for breeding and has produced a number of fine quality hybrids in brilliant hues, greatly widening the appeal of these popular windowsill gems. *P. speciosa* is typical of the genus with its widespread petals and sepals and generously colored lip, gaily patterned with yellow striations and red dots. A single flower is usually produced but occasionally two will open on the stem; the blooms last for about ten days.

Flower: 6cm (2 1/2 in) wide
Plant: 12cm (5in) high
Pan size: 5cm (2in) deep

Pleione Shantung 'Ridgeway' AM/RHS (left)

This beautiful apricot-colored hybrid is the result of crossing two species, the well-known *P. formosana*, which has pink and white forms, with the lesser-known *P. confusa*, the only yellow species in the genus. Originally known as *P. forrestii*, this latter species was collected in southwest China in 1904 by the plant collector George Forrest. Until recently only a single clone was in cultivation, and this was proving difficult to grow and to breed. But in the late 1970s, further clones were bred and the breeding qualities of the species were realized, with the raising of such hybrids as Shantung, produced in 1977. The rich yellow of this species has been combined with a pink form of *P. formosana* to produce Shantung's lovely apricot coloring.

Flower: 8cm (3in) wide
Plant: 15cm (6in) high
Pan size: 10cm (4in) deep

pseudobulbs. Place the bulbils in a paper bag for the winter to repot in spring. During winter, while the dormant bulbs are resting, leave completely dry and take them out of the pan or place it on a high, light shelf where they can stay until spring reactivates their growth. Overwinter these plants anywhere light and frost-free. They do not need the same minimum winter night temperatures as other cool-growing orchids: 5–7°C (41–45°F) suits them well.

During their summer growing season, pleiones are intolerant of high temperatures and need to be kept very cool at night, with daytime temperatures not exceeding 24°C (75°F). Where conditions are favorable, grow pleiones outdoors in a suitable bed or in containers sunk in the ground, bringing them back indoors for the winter. Otherwise, grow them indoors on a cool windowsill or in an unheated cold frame; they look best when the pseudobulbs are grown in quantity and their real character shines through. Try to maintain the size of the pseudobulbs each year. If these become reduced and the plants stop flowering, they could be in a spot that is too warm, or have been given insufficient water while developing.

A few fall-blooming species, including *P. praecox* and *P. maculata*, grow during winter, resting in summer and flowering in fall, so their growing season is reversed from the norm. Amateurs often start with *P. formosana* and think that all the plants in this genus will be equally easy to grow but in fact other pleiones can be slow-growing and need specialist care and attention to detail. In any case, the upsurge of interest has been among the spring-blooming hybrids, created by the lovely colors available.

Pleione Tongariro (below)

This hybrid, which shows a strong resemblance to the original species, is a cross between Versailles (*P. formosana* x *P. limprichtii*) and *P. speciosa*. Versailles was the first to be produced in the genus and since 1963, when it first flowered, numerous further hybrids have been made, greatly raising the profile of these pretty orchids. Although Versailles itself was raised in France, almost all the later hybrids have been produced in Britain by Ian Butterfield, who has made this delightful genus his specialty. Many of his hybrids carry the names of well-known volcanoes. There are several named clones of this hybrid that vary only slightly in the intensity of their coloring; all are extremely pretty.

Flower: 6cm (2 1/2 in) wide
Plant: 12cm (5in) high
Pan size: 5cm (2in) deep

Pleione formosana var. semi-alba (above)

This is probably the best known of the species and among the easiest to grow; in sheltered areas it can be raised outdoors in a specially prepared bed. The species is similar to *P. speciosa,* and many hybrids have been produced with one or both as a starting point. Because *P. formosana* is extremely variable, with many color variations, carefully selective breeding has enabled a wide range of colors to be produced among its hybrids. While the best clones command high prices, the more ordinary ones are still desirable; it can often be found in outlets other than specialist nurseries, sold unpotted and unestablished. This variety has glistening white sepals and petals, with discreet yellow and brown lip coloring. A pure white variety is also found, devoid of coloring on the lip. It is not unusual for this plant to produce two flowers on a stem.

Flower: 6cm (2 1/2 in) wide
Plant: 12cm (5in) high
Pan size: 5cm (2in) deep

Pleione Etna (below)

This is a primary hybrid, raised in Britain in 1979 from the Chinese species, *P. speciosa* and *P. limprichtii*, which are closely related and look similar. Etna therefore shows little difference from the species but has inherited vigor while retaining gloriously bright coloring. This hybrid is also important for the genus because both species are available from very few clones and this further breeding has enabled nurseries to bring a much wider range into cultivation. The flower is slightly smaller than that of *P. speciosa* and resembles its other parent in this respect. Etna makes a perfect "first orchid" and a single

pseudobulb will multiply rapidly to provide a whole panful within a few years. *P. limprichtii,* in cultivation since 1934, is covered with snow in the wild during the coldest part of the year.

Flower: 6cm (2 1/2 in) wide
Plant: 12cm (5in) high
Pan size: 5cm (2in) deep

other cool-growing orchids

The previous pages have covered some of the most exciting orchids in popular cultivation. There are, however, many more examples of cool-growing orchids that are as varied as they are numerous, but they are generally less readily available than those sold for houseplant culture. To the inexperienced eye, some are unrecognizable as orchids, but they serve to illustrate the wide variation between different species and genera. The following entries give a brief taste of miscellaneous other orchids, several of which have devotees among enthusiasts for their ease of cultivation, the compactness of their growth, and, above all, their delightful flowers, which offer their own unique variations of beauty. These orchids will take a little more searching for, but you can find such gems in specialist nurseries, on display at orchid exhibitions, and in the collections of enthusiasts; all will enhance your knowledge of the vast orchid kingdom.

This selection has been chosen from among literally hundreds for their special beauty. Being mostly small in stature, they will be quite at home on the windowsill, growing in humidity trays where their requirements can be met easily. These plants usually are available as young, flowering-sized specimens, or they may be bought as new young plants that will require some growing before their full potential is reached. Within a few years, small plants can become established as mature specimens with a true identity. Other plants bought when small may, over the years, become surprisingly large and, if they outgrow their allotted space, may have to be divided up into smaller pieces once again. In this way you can regulate the size of your orchids as well as increase your collection. Be aware that some small plants can produce very long flowering spikes, which may make them more difficult to accommodate in the home. With careful planning you can arrange your collection to ensure that you have one or two orchids in bloom at various months, to create interest all year-round. By buying plants when they are in flower, you can be sure of the individual's flowering time as well as other aspects of its blooming. Details of cultivation are given for each individual entry.

Trichopilia tortilis (above) grows in the tropical rain forests of South America. The neat plants, with oval pseudobulbs and a single leaf, produce one or two dramatic flowers on a slender spike in spring or early summer. The long, narrow petals and sepals twist along their length to give these plants the common name of "corkscrew orchid." The lip is closed at the top but flares out dramatically to a circular white globe with a deep yellow center. This is an easy orchid to grow in pots or mounted on cork bark, as here.

Brassia Rex (right) is one of the distinctive spider orchids with narrow, elongated petals and sepals. See page 115 for a full entry.

Brassia verrucosa (this page)

Brassias, known as spider orchids for their amazingly long, narrow petals and sepals, are exciting orchids to grow. This South American epiphytic species is the most prized in the genus for its light green sprays of delightfully fragrant flowers, which may be up to six or eight on a stem. The plants resemble robust odontoglossums, to which they are closely related and with which they will interbreed in certain combinations. In multigeneric hybrids, however, the length of the flower parts is never so great, and much of the original charm of this species is lost. The flowers appear in early summer and last for about three weeks.

Flower: 15cm (6in) long
Flower spike: 30cm (12in) long
Plant: 25cm (10in) high
Pot size: 18cm (7in)
Watering: Well in summer, less in winter
Position: Light shade in summer, full light in winter
Temperature: 10°C (50°F) min., 30°C (86°F) max.

Brassia Rex (above)

Though not a large genus, the brassias are represented in many mixed collections by a few of the species and their hybrids, such as Rex. They are probably most distinctive and easily recognizable by their spiderlike flowers, which produce extremely long and narrow petals and sepals. In this hybrid, the sepals and petals have been further extended, with bold brown patterning on the green base. The lip, also elongated, is white to creamy white, and decorated with brown dotting. These sweetly scented flowers are produced on long, arching flower spikes in early summer. The plants are neat growers, resembling the odontoglossums with which they will readily interbreed to produce bigeneric hybrids, mostly with *Oncidium* and *Miltonia*.

Flower: 20cm (8in) long
Flower spike: 30cm (12in) long
Plant: 20cm (8in) high
Pot size: 15cm (6in)
Watering: Well in summer, less in winter
Position: Light shade in summer, full light in winter
Temperature: 10°C (50°F) min., 30°C (86°F) max.

Thunia marshalliana (this page)
Thunias are great fun to grow. This popular species is one of no more than six in a tiny genus native to India, China, and Southeast Asia. They produce tall, fleshy canes, or pseudobulbs, leafed along their length with soft-textured, narrowly oval leaves. They start their new growth in early spring and grow at a fast rate through the summer, flowering from the top of the completed cane to produce a cascading spray of foaming flowers. The blooms, produced in short succession and lasting weeks at a time, have pure white petals and sepals, their deeply frilled and hairy lip overlaid with golden yellow or rosy pink. After flowering, the canes mature and all the foliage is shed. In winter, the canes can be left in their pots, or taken out and placed in trays. Repot early in the new year, when new growth is seen at the base; the old canes will shrivel and die.

Flower: 20cm (8in) wide
Plant: 60cm (24in) high
Pot size: 15cm (6in)
Watering: Well in summer; keep dry in winter
Position: Shade in summer, full light in winter
Temperature: 10°C (50°F) min., 30°C (86°F) max.

Anguloa uniflora (below)

The anguloas are a small genus known as the cradle orchids because of their loosely hinged lip at the center of the cupped bloom, which rocks back and forth when the flower is moved from side to side. The other common name is tulip orchid, a reference to its cupped or tulip shape. This species comes from South America, having been discovered in Peru in 1798, growing at high altitudes in the Andes; it first flowered in cultivation in 1842. The tall, robust plants produce oval pseudobulbs with several wide, ribbed leaves, which are shed for the winter when the plant is dormant. Activity starts in the spring, the new growths developing alongside the flower spike, which terminates in a single white bloom whose large petals and sepals are peppered on the inside with deep pink. A mature plant will produce multiple flowers in one season. Anguloas are related to lycastes, with which they will interbreed to produce a bigeneric hybrid genus, *Angulocaste*, including some of the largest flowers among popular orchids.

Flower: 5cm (2in) wide
Plant: 50cm (20in) high
Pot size: 15cm (6in)
Watering: Well in summer; keep dry in winter
Position: Light shade in summer, full light in winter
Temperature: 10°C (50°F) min., 30°C (86°F) max.

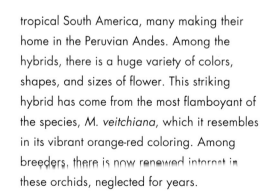

Masdevallia Whiskers (above)

These charming, mysterious little orchids are among the greatest characters in the orchid family. Their neat, epiphytic plants produce tufted stems and leaves and their triangular-shaped flowers, which may be single or several on a stem, are made up from grossly enlarged and partially fused sepals, often with long tails. The insignificant petals and lip are hidden away at the center of the bloom. Their distinctive shape has earned them the common name of kite orchids. Masdevallias like to be kept evenly moist all year-round, never becoming too wet at the roots. Their flowering time is various, but mainly during the summer months. The numerous and varied species within the genus come from a wide area of tropical South America, many making their home in the Peruvian Andes. Among the hybrids, there is a huge variety of colors, shapes, and sizes of flower. This striking hybrid has come from the most flamboyant of the species, *M. veitchiana*, which it resembles in its vibrant orange-red coloring. Among breeders, there is now renewed interest in these orchids, neglected for years.

Flower: 4cm (1½in) wide
Plant: 15cm (6in) high
Pot size: 10cm (4in)
Watering: Lightly all year
Position: Good shade in summer, less in winter
Temperature: 10°C (50°F) min., 24°C (75°F) max.

Stanhopea maculosa (left)

The stanhopeas are truly amazing orchids, widely distributed throughout South and Central America, where they grow epiphytically on stout branches in forest areas. Their large, ribbed pseudobulbs are topped by a single thick, leathery leaf, but their most unusual feature is that they produce their large fleshy flowers on spikes that hang below the plant, or that burrow down through the potting material to emerge underneath. For this reason they are always grown in hanging baskets, either open slatted wooden types, or plastic aquatic net pots, which enables the flower spike to push out through the bottom of the container. The spikes emerge in summer and carry some of the most curiously shaped of all orchid flowers; these are richly colored and highly fragrant, but last for three to four days only. The base of the lip carries two horn-like projections, which assist the pollinating insect to enter the flower at the right angle. These have given this orchid its common name of bull's horns orchid, or Toro, Toro!—the large red splashes on the petals are said to be the blood of the bull. The flowers need to be viewed sideways to discern the unique shape of their petals, sepals, and lip.

Flower: 8cm (3in) wide
Plant: 20cm (8in) high
Pot size: 12cm (5in)
Watering: Well in summer, less in winter
Position: Light shade in summer, full light in winter
Temperature: 10°C (50°F) min., 30°C (86°F) max.

Gongora galeata (below)

This is one of the smaller-growing species within an extraordinary genus. Introduced around 1830 from Mexico, it underwent several name changes before being included in this genus in 1854. The attractive plants have ribbed, cone-shaped pseudobulbs with a pair of medium green leaves. The slender, wirelike flower spikes produce several orange-scented flowers during the summer, ranging in color from yellow-green to buff brown. In times past many more gongoras were grown, but today the species are rarely seen. With very little hybridizing having been done between the species, only a few species remain in cultivation.

Flower: 4cm (1 1/2 in) wide
Plant: 20cm (8in) high
Pot size: 12cm (5in)
Watering: Well in summer, less in winter
Position: Light shade in summer, full light in winter
Temperature: 10°C (50°F) min., 30°C (86°F) max

Gongora maculata (right)

These orchids are among the most weird, producing strange-looking flowers on pendent spikes that hang loosely over the edge of their pot. The main colors represented are yellow, orange-yellow, yellow-green, and buff brown. The long flower spikes of this species carry over a dozen light, fanciful flowers, resembling a flock of birds in flight. Individually, the petals are thrown back behind the flower, while the lip remains at right angles to it; the dorsal sepal protrudes above the column. The summer-blooming flowers are usually strongly scented. Cone-shaped pseudobulbs carry a pair of ribbed leaves and aerial roots are often an impressive feature. The plants vary in size, but the majority are most easily grown in a greenhouse, where they do well grown in hanging baskets suspended near the glass.

Flower: 4cm (1 1/2 in) wide
Plant: 20cm (8in) high
Pot size:12cm (5in)
Watering: Well in summer, less in winter
Position: Light shade in summer, full light in winter
Temperature: 10°C (50°F) min., 30°C (86°F) max.

interm

Wherever you can offer a few extra degrees of heat in winter, a whole new range of orchids opens up. Intermediate-growing orchids need temperatures ranging from a minimum of 13°C (55°F) on winter nights to a summer daytime maximum of 30°C (86°F). A number of them will grow alongside the cool-growing orchids for most of the year, but they need the extra warmth on winter nights. By making only small adjustments to a growing area, you should be able to create a suitable environment for the warmer types. A few extra degrees at night can easily be achieved by moving them to a room in the house that is naturally warmer, or where you maintain a little background heating overnight. Another possibility is to divide off a section of greenhouse where there is enough room, without creating too confining a division.

Separating cool-growing orchids from intermediates during the winter ensures that both groups are grown in a temperature range that suits them; keeping them together in the hope that all will thrive will result in some doing much better than others. Cool-growing orchids kept warmer at night to suit the intermediates may not bloom because they need the nighttime drop of a few degrees to initiate flowering. Keep a maximum–minimum thermometer in each of the different growing areas, to be sure of giving your orchids the temperature range they need.

ediate

orchids

the cattleya alliance

Underlining the many natural and man-made genera horticulturally referred to as cattleyas is a complex web of interwoven hybrids comprising the largest group of related plants in the orchid family. As well as the naturally occurring *Cattleya* and *Laelia*, there are the man-made genera, of which the most notable are *Sophrolaeliocattleya* (incorporating the small brightly colored *Sophronitis*) and *Brassolaeliocattleya* with the large-flowered green *Brassavola* (now *Rhyncholaelia*). Other combinations have created a colossal variation, but we restrict this section to those cattleyas popular for their ease of culture and availability.

Cattleyas and laelias are the two natural genera that appear most often in cultivation. Evergreen cattleyas produce pseudobulbs, from short (10cm/4in) to tall (1m/39in), along a visible strong rhizome. They are mainly club-shaped and sheathed, and support either one leaf (unifoliate) or two (bifoliate). Both

types produce rigid, oval to long leaves that are thick and leathery, while the flower spikes come from the apex of the pseudobulb at the base of the leaves. The short stems carry one to six large blooms up to 12cm (5in) across. They are among the most fabulous of all cultivated orchids. They are highly fragrant, and their subtle colorings include crisp white, buttercup yellow, and the gorgeous hues of pink-purple, rich mauve, and lavender, all with the colorful lip combinations at which these orchids excel.

The laelias are a similar genus, producing elongated, often slender pseudobulbs to 30cm (12in) tall and a single oval, leathery leaf. Flower spikes, up to 30cm (12in) long, extend from the top of the pseudobulb and support up to eight attractive flowers in a similar color range to that of the cattleyas. Most species within these two genera are fall- or spring-flowering, their blooms lasting three weeks in perfection; the large-flowered types require some support (see page 124) to be seen at their best. For the beginner there is a multitude of colorful hybrids to choose from, all retaining the delicious scent that typifies this alliance, while for the connoisseur there are the increasingly rare and much sought-after, lovely but vulnerable species, which need to be carefully tended.

Laeliocattleya **Persepolis (right) is a bigeneric hybrid combining the qualities of** *Cattleya* **and** *Laelia* **to produce an outstanding flower with the full** *Cattleya* **shape and attractive, delicate coloring on the petals and sepals. A more dramatically colored clone of this plant is shown (left) in close-up. See page 129 for a full entry.**

Origins

Cattleyas were among the first tropical orchids to come into cultivation, being highly prized for their large blooms. The species range through tropical South America, across the Isthmus of Panama, as far north as the rain forests of Mexico, but the best are found in the steamy Brazilian rain forests. The epiphytic plants grow on the trunks and stout branches of the forest trees, in their wild state existing for hundreds of years, growing into huge clumps several meters across.

While the number of *Cattleya* species is comparatively small, they are so closely related to other genera in the alliance that much interbreeding has taken place, resulting in many intergeneric hybrids. The first *Cattleya* cross appeared in 1857. Called *Cattleya* Hybrida, it was the first tropical hybrid to be recognized by the Royal Horticultural Society in Britain, which awarded it a first class certificate. During the first half of the twentieth century, cattleyas were in demand as cut flowers, and today they are cultivated by a growing band of devotees. Due to their size and irregular flowering habits, they have not entered the potted plant trade in large numbers, but will be found in specialty nurseries.

Laeliocattleya Drumbeat (right)
This bigeneric hybrid genus is the result of a combination of *Laelia* and *Cattleya*, first made in 1887. Many such crosses have been made over the years, producing fine large-flowered varieties that display lush colorings on showy blooms, which may be white, yellow, or shades of lavender-pink or purple. Some of these hybrids are spring-blooming, while others produce their flowers in the fall; hybrids may take their flowering cue from one parent or the other. The delightful fragrance is maintained in hybridization in this alliance, and in some hybrids is even enhanced. This well-rounded, frilled bloom is the result of selective breeding to combine various outstanding qualities.

Flower: 15cm (6in) wide
Plant: 38cm (15in) high
Pot size: 15cm (6in)

Laelia Pulcherrima (above)
This is a modern version of a much older cross first made over 100 years ago between two Brazilian species, *Laelia purpurata* (introduced in 1852 and still very popular in collections) and the lesser-known, but equally attractive, *L. lobata*. Today's hybrid looks considerably different from the 1898 cross, because other clones of the species have been used, creating a distinct and beautiful new hybrid that retains the original name. The wide flower has the typical open shape associated with many laelias, an extremely variable genus, while the lip is distinctly trumpet-shaped, flared at the end and richly colored. The pseudobulbs are long and slender with a solitary leaf.

Flower: 18cm (7in) wide
Plant: 60cm (24in) high
Pot size: 20cm (8in)

Cultivation

Cattleyas like to be comfortable at all times, so balancing the temperature with humidity and moisture at the roots is the key to growing these exuberant orchids successfully. Use an open, swiftly draining potting mixture made up of coarse bark, with an inert man-made material added to absorb water. Water cattleyas well while they are growing and fertilize regularly every second or third watering. They like plenty of light, but not direct sunlight. Although their foliage looks tough, their leaves will burn easily if exposed to sun, so shade them well in summer and give full light in winter.

When the buds first emerge from the top of the pseudobulb, they are enclosed by a green sheath; as they grow, they burst out from the sheath, splitting it along its length. It can be some weeks between the development of the sheath and the emergence of the buds, during which time the sheath may become brown and wither, as it has a short lifespan; this will not affect the developing buds. Occasionally, the sheath fails to split, trapping the buds inside. You could, as a precaution, slit open the top of the sheath. When the buds are left to open naturally, the flowers assume a nodding position and where there are two or more on the stem, they will crowd each other out. To prevent this, each bloom can be individually held in position by a slim bamboo cane. Cut each cane to a length where it will reach to just above the stem behind each flower when pushed into the potting mix. Make a split in the top of each one, about 2cm (1in) long. Push a cane into the pot, then carefully ease the flower stem into the slit; the cane will hold the flower firmly, without damaging it. You can now position the flower by twisting the cane in either direction. Do this with all the flowers until the best position is reached, being careful not to snap the stems. Alternatively you can use horticultural string to tie each bloom to its support.

The roots of *Cattleya* are white, thick, and rigid, and they start to develop long after the new growth has started. The plants have two main growing seasons, spring and fall, when the new roots will be active. When new roots start to grow, they produce an explosion of green tips at the base of the latest pseudobulb. Until they enter the potting material they are vulnerable to

damage and injury from slugs or snails. If the last pseudobulb has been made outside the rim of the pot, the roots will progress down the outside of it, becoming aerial. For this reason, it is advisable to repot cattleyas after the new growth has started but before the new roots are produced.

Hybrid cattleyas become large and bulky and are easiest to cope with in a greenhouse where they have plenty of space and high humidity. They enjoy light overhead spraying in summer, but avoid getting water droplets on the flowers, which will cause spotting of the paper-thin petals and sepals. If you grow cattleyas indoors, select compact varieties and give as much filtered light as possible all year-round. In tropical countries, they do well in the protection of a shade house, which allows a flow of fresh air at all times. Cattleyas need a minimum of 13°C (55°F) on winter nights. When exposed to prolonged lower temperatures, their growth suffers, and ailments such as black spot can occur through being cold and damp. Because much of the plant is covered with sheaths, cattleyas are prone to harbor scale insects, so when the sheaths have withered and dried, peel them off, checking for these insects (see page 217). Cattleyas can rest for weeks at a time, so when there is no sign of active growth, water just enough to prevent the pseudobulbs from shriveling. When large enough, they can be divided (see page 209).

Laeliocattleya Veldorado 'Polka' AM/RHS (below)

The diversity of flower color is well illustrated in this superb, French-bred modern *Cattleya* hybrid, raised in 1976 from Amber Glow and Colibri. One to three flowers can be produced on the spike, the rich yellow petals and sepals contrasting vividly with the deep mauve lip, shot through with gold veining toward the throat. The blooms also carry a sweet fragrance.

This medium-sized plant has a single, semi-rigid leaf and blooms once a year when the season's pseudobulb is completed. The usual flowering time is fall. To encourage the flowers to live longer, place out of strong light while in bloom and keep on the dry side.

Flower: 12cm (5in) wide
Plant: 38cm (15in) high
Pot size: 15cm (6in)

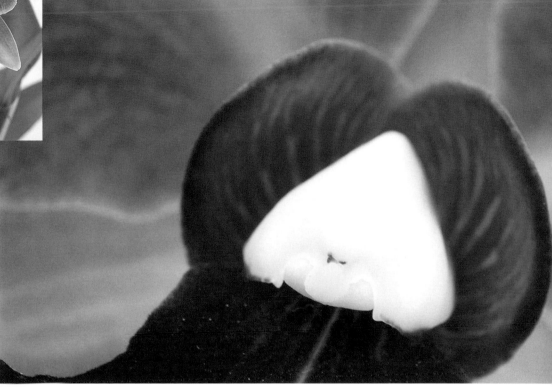

Laeliocattleya Elizabeth Fulton
'La Tuilerie' AM/RHS (above & right)

Raised in 1977 in the U.S. from Amber Glen and the Brazilian species *Cattleya bicolor*, this richly colored hybrid is the result of generations of selective breeding to bring out all the qualities exhibited in its flower. The coppery coloring, rarely seen among cattleyas, is a welcome addition to an already extensive color range. The sepals and petals display the ideal shape looked for in this genus and the exquisitely self-colored lip is a perfect complement to them. The plant is a neat grower, its slender pseudobulbs carrying a single leaf, with the blooms appearing well above the foliage. One to three flowers may be expected, the usual number being two, and these appear in autumn.

Flower: 12cm (5in) wide
Plant: 38cm (15in) high
Pot size: 15cm (6in)

Sophrolaeliocattleya Rocket Burst
'Deep Enamel' AM/RHS (below)

Among the *Cattleya* alliance is the small genus *Sophronitis*, containing just four species. The best of these produces a small, vivid red flower and the whole plant is less than 15cm (6in) in bloom. When the red species *S. coccinea* is crossed with a larger, small-flowered *Laelia* or *Cattleya*, the result is deeply colored hybrids such as Rocket Burst, awarded on both sides of the Atlantic for its exquisitely vibrant coloring and star-shaped flowers. It blooms in spring and lasts up to four weeks.

Flower: 5cm (2in) wide
Plant: 30cm (12in) high
Pot size: 15cm (6in)

Cattleya Hawaiian Wedding Song (left)
In this American-raised white hybrid, which is
pure *Cattleya*, the petals have become so
frilled and enlarged that their shape is almost
undefined, causing the flower to lose some of
the roundness that is the hallmark of quality
among these lovely hybrids. The lip is well
defined, however, and exhibits a perfectly
frilled edge and deep yellow throat. This
modern hybrid is from the unifoliate group,
producing one leathery oval leaf, and was
registered in 1982 from the parents Angel
Bells and Claesiana, in Hawaii. Angel Bells
comes from Empress Bells and Little Angel,
raised in 1960 from the famous stud plant
Bow Bells, while Claesiana is an older,
English-bred primary hybrid raised in 1916
from the species *C. intermedia* and
C. loddigesii.

Flower: 12cm (5in) wide
Plant: 38cm (15in) high
Pot size: 15cm (6in)

Flamboyant and exotic-looking, cattleyas deserve their popular name of "chocolate-box orchids."

Cattleya Little Miss Charming (below)
Raised along different breeding lines, this attractive hybrid is an example of the variety to be found among the _Cattleya_ genus. Here the flower is spaced out, the petals and sepals narrower and neither touching nor overlapping as in the rounder flowers. Two to three blooms are produced on a longer stem, while the pseudobulbs are tall and slender with a single long, oval leaf. The parents of this American-raised hybrid, registered in 1984, are Snowberry and the species, _C. loddigesii_. Since Snowberry already has this species as one of its parents, the dominant genes are from _C. loddigesii_, as can be seen in both the flower shape and growth habit of Little Miss Charming.

Flower: 10cm (4in) wide
Plant: 30cm (12in) high
Pot size: 15cm (6in)

Laeliocattleya Persepolis (above)
The parents of this 1973-registered bigeneric hybrid are _Cattleya_ Kitiwake and _Laelia_ Pegi Mayne; it was raised in the U.S. from a line of similar crosses. The lip shows a marked _Cattleya_ influence and, with its rich magenta coloring, provides an ideal contrast for this winning color combination. This is an important breeding plant that has gone on to produce mainly summer-blooming white-flowered hybrids. The plant is strong and robust with a thick leathery leaf. During the winter these orchids like all the light available, but early spring sunshine can quickly burn through their tender leaf structures, so they should always be given some shade, or moved to a shadier place, from spring onward, once the sun starts to gain power.

Flower: 15cm (6in) wide
Plant: 38cm (15in) high
Pot size: 15cm (6in)

Epicattleya Siam Jade (below)

The epidendrums are a genus closely related to the cattleyas and help to make up the *Cattleya* alliance. When selected epidendrums are crossed with cattleyas some startlingly different colored plants emerge, as with this beautiful, clear-green, American-bred hybrid. The sepals and petals are more thickly textured than those of other cattleyas and the attractive cream lip is almost rigid. This plant is small and compact, the pseudobulbs being shortened. Its flowering season is various, the flowers blooming most often in spring.

Flower: 5cm (2in) wide
Plant: 10cm (4in) high
Pot size: 10cm (4in)

Epicattleya El Hatillo 'Santa Maria' (above)

This American-raised hybrid combines the qualities of two genera to produce an endearing flower. It is a primary hybrid from *Cattleya mossiae* and *Encyclia tampense*, the former being an earlier introduction from Venezeula, described in 1836. It first flowered in the collection of Mrs. Moss in 1838 and today can be found in most, if not all, modern *Cattleya* hybrids. In this cross the *Encyclia* has proved to be the dominant parent, influencing the overall flower shape, while the vivid lip coloring is typical of many cattleyas. The neat-growing plant has slender, elongated pseudobulbs supporting a pair of narrow, rigid leaves, from between which the flower spike emerges. This grows upright and carries four to five fragrant flowers, colored a light creamy green, with a brightly contrasting lip. The plant likes to be warm and provided with good light throughout the year.

Flower: 5cm (2in) wide
Plant: 20cm (8in) high
Pot size: 12cm (5in)

Cattleya Sir Jeremiah Colman (above)

In the search for the elusive blue in cattleyas, this plant is a winner. An older hybrid that still retains its classic status, it was raised in the U.S. in 1976 and named in honor of Sir Jeremiah Colman, an eminent breeder of blue-flowered *Cattleya* hybrids during the first half of the twentieth century. The blue coloring is obtained from the *coerulea* form of several *Cattleya* and *Laelia* species, and this plant has proved to be an excellent breeder, producing further blue varieties over the years. Its sepals and petals are light eggshell blue, the frilled lip is mauve around the edge and yellow at the center. A neat grower, its slender pseudobulbs have a pair of narrow oval leaves at the apex.

Flower: 9cm (3 1/2 in) wide
Plant: 30cm (12in) high
Pot size: 12cm (5in)

dendrobiums

The dendrobiums are an immense genus existing in many parts of the world, their species showing great variation depending on the country of origin (see page 102 for a general description). From Northern Australia and New Guinea come many ornate and distinct kinds, several uncommon in cultivation in other parts of the world. But there is one group, collectively known as *Phalaenopsis*-type dendrobiums because of the likeness of their flowers to those of the genus *Phalaenopsis*, popular for the amateur grower. Starting with the highly variable species, *D. bigibbum*, and others related to it, many colorful hybrids have been bred, all of which will grow in an intermediate greenhouse. Their culture is like that for cooler-growing Indian dendrobiums (see page 105).

Phalaenopsis-type dendrobiums produce elongated, hard-caned pseudobulbs, with pairs of dark green, stiffened leaves along their length. They bloom from the top half of the leading cane, producing long stems that support a dozen or more showy flowers. These are usually rounded in shape, all parts of equal size, in colors ranging from white, through shades of light yellow to incredibly rich mauve and purple combinations. The flowers are mostly self-colored, or they may be more deeply tinged toward the petal tips.

In cultivation these plants like high light levels, combined with warmth (minimum winter temperature 13°C/55°F) and humidity. In spring, when the plants are flowering and producing new growths, give plenty of water at the roots; keep them in a small pot (10cm/4in unless otherwise stated), and fertilize regularly in summer. Daytime temperatures can go as high as 30°C (86°F), provided the humidity is well balanced. Give just enough shading to prevent the leaves from

Dendrobium miyakei (below)
A pretty species from the Philippines, *D. miyakei* produces long pendent canes which are leafed along their length; it retains some foliage throughout the year. The attractive rosy mauve flowers are produced from side nodes along the canes and appear in a drooping truss of clustered blooms in spring, following a dry winter's rest period. During the summer, it likes to be well sprayed and kept moist while the long canes are developing; good light is another important factor in ensuring a show of flowers. This species was quite rare in cultivation until recent years, when it became more freely available from nursery-raised stock. It blooms and reblooms from the older, leafless canes, when these have matured. It is best grown in a hanging basket, close to the glass.

Flower: 1cm (¹/₂ in) wide
Plant: 30cm (12in) high
Pot size: 12cm (5in)

Dendrobium victoria-regina (above left)
This species is closely related to *D. miyakei* (see right) which it resembles in habit; both species come from the Philippines and grow on trees as epiphytes. *D. victoria-regina* has slender canes that become deciduous after two to three years. As they mature, they assume a pendent position, which is why they are best cultivated in pots or small baskets suspended above the staging, where their natural habit can be allowed to develop. Alternatively, the canes may be tied into an upright position, which does not affect flowering. Small, bluish mauve flowers are produced in clusters of two or three from midway to the top of the canes; several canes can bloom in one season. Good light is needed to prompt flowering.

Flower: 3cm (1¹/₄ in) wide
Plant: 30cm (12in) high
Pot size: 7cm (3in)
Temperature: 10°C (50°F) min., 30°C (86°F) max.

Dendrobium Thongchai Gold (above)
Further distinct breeding lines using Australian
and New Guinea species have made a huge
variety of colors and flower shapes available.
Many new hybrids are raised in Thailand,
where the climate ideally suits these plants.
The species behind Thongchai Gold includes

D. bigibbum, once known as D. phalaenopsis,
a variable species first described in 1852,
having been cultivated in Britain at the Royal
Botanic Gardens since 1824. Thongchai Gold
is one of a number that produce yellow-gold
flowers, the dark red-mauve lip a stunning
contrast. The petals, narrow at the base, are

rounded at their tips; the smaller sepals may
be lighter in color. The flowers are carried on
spikes produced from the top half of the canes.

Flower: 5cm (2in) wide
Plant: 30cm (12in) high
Pot size: 12cm (5in)

getting scorched. These orchids grow quickly, developing their canes within six months. Some can become extremely tall, with canes up to a meter (3 feet); they need plenty of headroom. As the plant completes its growth, gradually reduce watering at the same time as giving more light, allowing the plants a complete rest for the winter. Dendrobiums should remain evergreen, shedding a few leaves but retaining most for another year or two.

Dendrobium **Dale Takiguchi** (left)

This attractive *Phalaenopsis*-type hybrid illustrates the beauty of the clear, pale-colored flowers that can be produced by breeding from the white, or albino, forms of the species. This is one of the hard-caned dendrobiums whose tall canes, pointed at the top, can remain evergreen for two to three years. The oval leaves cover the top half of the canes only, unlike the *D. nobile*-type hybrids, which are leafed through their whole length. This plant blooms freely in the spring and summer months, producing its lovely flowers on arching sprays, which will last for several weeks in perfection. Unlike other dendrobiums, these hybrids do not grow excessively tall, which makes them good subjects for a position on a well-lit windowsill.

Flower: 6cm (2$^{1}/_{2}$ in) wide
Plant: 40cm (16in) high

Dendrobium **All Seasons Blue** (right)

All Seasons Blue is one of many hybrids raised from the Australian species of hard-caned dendrobiums. Their more rigid canes remain upright without staking, their flowers produced on spikes from a terminal node in fall. The equally proportioned sepals and petals are spread wide, while the lip is small and neat, of similar plain coloring. The parents of this beautiful hybrid, raised in Thailand in 1995, are Pinky Sem and Minnie.

Flower: 4cm (1$^{1}/_{2}$ in) wide
Plant: 30cm (12in) high
Temperature: 10°C (50°F) min., 30°C (85°F) max.

Dendrobium rhodostictum x atroviolaceum (above)

This is an unusual hybrid raised from distinctive New Guinea species. The small-growing plant produces club-shaped pseudobulbs with leathery terminal leaves and is compact enough for indoor cultivation. The extraordinary blooms, whitish with light spotting on the outside of the petals, sport a small, neat, light green lip. Up to six flowers, carried on a loose flower spike, will last for six months or more. The species

D. atroviolaceum was seen for the first time in 1890 when exhibited at the Royal Horticultural Show in London, the year of its introduction. This species, dominant in the cross shown here, and its hybrids are admired for their fragrant blooms, among the longest-lived of all cultivated orchids.

Flower: 3cm (1¹/₄in) wide
Plant: 30cm (12in) high

slipper orchids

Phragmipedium besseae (left) was only discovered in 1980, when its vibrant red coloring caused a sensation. See page 150 for a full entry.

To many people, slipper orchids are the most fascinating group of orchids to study. They are certainly the most diverse, having separated from the rest of the orchid family and developed their own distinct plant and flower structure. All carry their easily recognizable trademark, the pouch or slipper, which is a further modification of the third petal, or lip, as it appears in other orchids. Their foliage and their habit of growth are also unique. Originally we knew all slipper orchids as *Cypripedium*, but today they are divided into three separate groups: *Paphiopedilum*, *Phragmipedium*, and *Cypripedium*. While the first two groups of slipper orchids are warm-growing, the terrestrial cypripediums require much cooler conditions; cypripediums are not included here because they are extremely rare in cultivation, being occasionally found in specialist collections, which is where they belong.

Today all slipper orchids growing in the wild are considered endangered species and appear on the priority list of the authority for the Convention on International Trade in Endangered Species (CITES), a body set up in 1973 to protect and conserve the world's threatened fauna and flora. In effect, CITES ensures that no listed plant species can be imported or exported to anywhere in the world without a special licence proving that the plant has been nursery-raised and is not a wild-collected specimen. Though the wild-collection of slipper orchids is totally banned, this protection unfortunately does not ensure their continuation in the wild, so great are the pressures on their natural habitats from man's activities, including poaching. Only those plants that survive in the most remote and inaccessible places of the world can be considered entirely safe from habitat destruction. It could even be claimed that the best protected plants are those now growing in botanical gardens, nature reserves, and national parks, where it is hoped that they will continue to exist as they have done in their natural habitats for thousands of years.

This close-up (right) of the pouch of the slipper orchid *Paphiopedilum* Jersey Freckles shows its extraordinary shape and elaborate patterning. See page 142 for a full entry.

paphiopedilums

Paphiopedilums were one of the first tropical orchids to be widely cultivated, and today they are still the most popular of the slipper orchids. These evergreen orchids, mainly terrestrial in the wild, produce growths consisting of two or more long and narrow, or oval, leaves, with each new growth arising from the base of the previous one. Many species compensate for the lack of pseudobulbs by producing thicker, fleshy leaves whose foliage is medium to dark green or mottled with lighter green; some leaves exhibit delicately peppered purple undersides. When the season's growth is completed, the flower bud emerges from the center. Compared to other orchids, their rooting system is sparse, the roots being brown and hairy. The plants vary in size from 8cm (3in) tall, or 15–30cm (6–12in) when in flower, to taller-growing types that may be 30cm (12in) tall in growth, with a flower spike twice that height.

Their flowers can last up to ten weeks, or longer where the sequential blooming of anything up to a dozen flowers in succession extends the flowering. Paphiopedilums also have the prettiest leaves of any orchid, and many are rewarding to grow for this attribute alone; the mottled-leaved varieties make very attractive houseplants.

Origins

Paphiopedilums are found growing in a wide variety of environments. They are equally at home in high mountain outcrops exposed to almost full sun as they are at sea level, where they cling to limestone cliffs, regularly catching the sea-salt spray at high tides. In between these extremes, we find them growing in dense jungle, mostly as terrestrials, but occasionally as epiphytes in the forks of trees. Their distribution extends from southern China, down through India, Myanmar, Malaysia, Borneo, and as far south as New Guinea, covering most of the islands of the Philippines in between. Many of these islands have evolved their own distinctive species and, surprisingly, new ones are still being found. There are also instances of old species, discovered by the Victorian explorers over a hundred years ago and since lost to cultivation, having been rediscovered in the last few years. Countries, including Vietnam and China, previously closed to the western world, have revealed some exciting finds among slipper orchids, which have led to some amazing new

Paphiopedilum Deperle (above) This is an extremely popular primary hybrid between the Vietnam species *P. delenatii* and the recently discovered Sumatran species, *P. primulinum*. The latter species, described only in 1973, has opened up a new breeding line for small yellow-flowered hybrids and has proved the dominant parent in this 1980 French-bred plant. The compact blooms of Deperle open one at a time in spring; they resemble those of *P. primulinum* in overall shape, and their coloring—a delightful soft, buttery yellow—belies the other parent, which usually passes its pink pigment on to its progeny.

Flower: 6cm (2^1/$_2$in) wide
Flower spike: 25cm (10in) long
Plant: 15cm (6in) high

Paphiopedilum Prime Child (below)

This unusual-looking hybrid has been raised from the Borneo species *P. rothschildianum*, noted for its extraordinary long and narrow petals. The downward-swooping petals of Prime Child are spotted along their length. While the species produces multiflowering spikes, this hybrid flowers in succession like its other parent, *P. primulinum*, with one bud (seen below and far left) opening at a time. The hybrid was originally raised in California in 1985; since then other nurseries have remade the cross, making it more widely available. Various clones show subtle differences in flower shape.

Flower: 18cm (7in) wide
Flower spike: 30cm (12in) long
Plant: 20cm (8in) high
Pot size: 12cm (5in)

hybrids. Though the export of *Paphiopedilum* species from their natural habitat is strictly controlled, even banned, this has not prevented new discoveries from being shipped round the world; prosecutions have taken place but the rewards for smuggling orchids seem to be worth the risk.

These slipper orchids are either tropical or subtropical. Some of the cooler-growing varieties come from species originating at high altitudes in the Himalayas. Cool-growing species, such as *P. insigne* and *P. spicerianum*, were among the first to be used for hybridizing. The first of the hybrids was raised in 1860 and some of the original crosses can still be found in nurseries around Europe, where the ageless charm of their flowers is highly prized. These hybrids were originally in great demand as cut flowers and grown by nurserymen in vast quantities for this purpose. But by the 1960s, the fashion had changed, and as heating costs soared and demand dropped, these plants were no longer found to be profitable. Many of the species have also proved difficult to raise from seed and are slow to reach maturity; it is not unusual to wait ten to twelve years before a *Paphiopedilum* flowers for the first time.

Several characteristics divide paphiopedilums into distinct horticultural groups, but they will all interbreed with each other, resulting in a huge hybrid group. Some of the South American phragmipediums are so similar in appearance to the Philippine and Borneo paphiopedilums that it is hard to believe they are incapable of interbreeding. But, to date, no intergeneric hybrids have been made between these two groups of slipper orchids or the cypripediums.

Paphiopedilum Chiquita (below)

This is another example of the new breed of paphiopedilums, using *P. primulinum* to bring in a different color range. This lime-yellow species, found in 1972 in Sumatra at the low altitude of 400m (1,300ft), was one of the best discoveries of that decade. It belongs to a small group of related species with narrow, wavy-edged petals and a distinctive pouch, traits that continue to characterize its hybrids. Here, light orange and peach shades are seen with the pale green dorsal sepal to give a pleasing combination. The light open flower shape is a contrast to the heavy rounded blooms seen in other varieties within the genus. Several flowers are produced at the end of the spike, but only one opens at a time.

Flower: 8cm (3in) wide
Flower spike: 15cm (6in) long
Plant: 13cm (5in) high

Types of Paphiopedilum

Among the most popular types are the Complex hybrids, producing long, narrow, plain green leaves and a single large, rounded bloom. The flower can be self-colored in peppery white, shining yellow, or through a multitude of rich shades between brown and red. Alternatively, they may be heavily spotted and striped, with two or more colors combined or overlaid to create a carnival of hues in high gloss. These wonderfully warm-toned flowers can last for months on the plant.

Then there is the Maudiae type of *Paphiopedilum*, single-flowered hybrids named after one of the first and most delightful hybrids made within this group. Their oval leaves are attractively mottled in green and grey-green, sometimes darkly peppered on the undersides, and their elegant flowers, carried proudly on tall, slender stems in summer, are either green or red. The green-flowered varieties are distinguished by their clear apple green coloring, with a striped dorsal sepal. The red-flowered kind, with flamed dorsal sepals, can almost border on black, some of them an amazingly dark, brooding purple in color; these have a great following as growers strive to produce the elusive all-black flower.

A number of sequential-flowering species have been hybridized to produce pretty compact blooms like those of *P.* Pinocchio (see opposite), probably the smallest in the genus. The plants have elongated, light green leaves, and the flowers appear on long stems, which gradually extend as buds open in succession over a period of several months. The main colorings in this group are clear shades of cornfield yellow and tan leading toward light orange, with a sprinkling of brown or purple. Bright and cheerful, these little plants have a captivating charm.

The last group, known as the *Rothschildianum* Group, have the most dramatically stunning flowers of all. These hybrids, raised from species that inhabit Borneo and the Philippines, have no equal. The flowers are distinguished by their extraordinary long, ribbonlike petals, which can extend almost vertically, or swivel horizontally for up to 15cm (6in). The plants are large and robust, their long leaves medium to dark green. In flower, their tall spikes may attain a height of a meter (3 feet) or more, the blooms, four to six on a stem, opening all together; they will remain on the plant for weeks during spring and summer, their coloring striking, almost unreal, combinations of near black and purple lines on a white base. While these dramatic plants are greatly sought after, unfortunately they are extremely slow to breed and to grow.

Paphiopedilum Pinocchio

(right)

Raised in France in 1977, this is a primary hybrid from two closely related species, *P. primulinum* and *P. glaucophyllum*. With its pretty, compact blooms, it is probably the smallest variety in the genus. The center of the bloom shows a deep green rostellum and on either side of the staminodium are the pollinia, hidden from view, but against which the pollinating insect must push to find its way out of the pouch. While these orchids do not eat or digest insects, they do trap them when they slip and fall into the pouch. The insect can easily escape, but in doing so either removes or deposits pollen.

Flower: 8cm (3in) wide
Flower spike: 25cm (10in) long
Plant: 15cm (6in) high

Cultivation

In cultivation the different paphiopedilums will all grow under one roof, which is surprising given that the species come from many different climates. With the occasional exception, their requirements are the same and a well-shaded greenhouse with a minimum winter nighttime temperature of 18°C (65°F) will suit them. Without pseudobulbs, they have no means of coping with long periods of drought, so keep them evenly moist all year-round, slightly drier in winter. The plants grow steadily, slowing down in winter but without having a true rest period. Pot into an open, well-drained potting material, using as small a pot as possible (10cm/4in unless otherwise stated). Complex types benefit from annual repotting, with as little disturbance to the root system as possible, often returning plants to the same size pot. Spray lightly in summer, but do not allow water to run down into the center of the growth, where it may cause rot.

Paphiopedilum Jersey Freckles (below)
This handsome Complex hybrid is typical of a multitude of similar varieties raised from Indian species such as *P. insigne*, *P. villosum*, and *P. barbatum*. Breeding continued over many generations to give rise to distinct colors and markings in the form of spots and dashes over a lighter base (see page 137 for a close-up detail of the lip). These hybrids have both cool- and warmer-growing varieties in their parental make-up. Jersey Freckles is a green-leafed type, which may be grown in a warm and shady position indoors or in a heated greenhouse. These plants dislike too much direct light and prefer the shadier places where the sun does not reach. A single flower, which can last for up to eight weeks, blooms during the winter months; a large specimen will produce more than one flower on separate stems from each new growth.

Flower: 12cm (5in) wide
Flower spike: 20cm (8in) long
Plant: 12cm (5in) high

Paphiopedilum villosum (above)
This cool-growing Himalayan species was discovered in 1853, growing epiphytically in the wet, mountainous areas of Burma (now Myanmar) at an altitude of 2,000m (6,560ft), where the nights are cool. In 1869 it was crossed with *P. barbatum*, a terrestrial Malaysian species with mottled foliage that grows at a lower altitude, to produce *P.* Harrisianum, the first hybrid in the genus. *P. villosum* has slender, dark green foliage and carries a single flower on the stem in late fall and winter. The color of polished brass, it has a high gloss to its waxy petals and pouch. This species has been used extensively in the past to produce many of today's fine hybrids, which still retain the shining colors and decoration on the dorsal sepal, but it is now less widely grown as the stock of cultivated plants dwindle, and it is no longer available from the wild.

Flower: 10cm (4in) wide
Flower spike: 15cm (6in) long
Plant: 25cm (10in) high
Position: Cool and shady
Temperature: 10°C (50°F) min., 24°C (75°F) max.

Paphiopedilum Silverlight (above)

Bred along similar lines to *P. Chiquita* (see page 140), this flower exhibits the buttery yellow color of *P. primulinum*, the original species from which it was raised. This group of sequential-flowering hybrids prefers a warmer environment, reflecting the original home of the dominant parent species; a low-altitude plant from Sumatra, their slender foliage is medium to light green, indicating their preference for shady conditions. Apart from yellow, light green and white varieties are seen in this new line of breeding, gaining popularity with those who prefer smaller flowers.

Flower: 8cm (3in) wide
Flower spike: 15cm (6in) tall
Plant: 12cm (5in) high

Paphiopedilum Gina Short (below)
Pink-flowered varieties of *Paphiopedilum* have
always been more unusual, but are much
admired and sought after. Pink coloring was
unknown in the genus until the accidental
discovery of *P. delenatii* in 1913 by a French
soldier fighting in Vietnam. The large flowers
usually retain their distinctive shape, with an
egg-shaped pouch typical of the species.
One to three summer-blooming flowers can
be produced on a single short flower spike.
These compact plants also produce exquisite
foliage, darkly tessellated on the surface with
purple peppering on the undersides of the
leaves. Keep the foliage dry because of the
danger of water lodging in the center, which
will rot the growth.

Flower: 10cm (4in) wide
Flower spike: 12cm (5in) long
Plant 12cm (5in) high

Paphiopedilum Holdenii (above)
There are a number of these clean, clear,
green-flowered types among the mottled-leaf
varieties of *Paphiopedilum* and all are
popular. The dorsal sepal carries the typical
stripes while the remainder of the flower is
self-colored. This is an older variety, raised
in Britain in 1909 from the green-flowered
P. callosum var. *sanderae* and *P. Maudiae*,
itself a *P. callosum* hybrid. It is still in demand
today, along with others that have been bred
from it. The attractive light green mottled
foliage is compact, with oval leaves. A single
bloom, produced on a tall stem, will need
the support of a thin bamboo cane to hold
the flower upright. Wait until the flower has
opened and become set for a few days
before tying it back to the cane so that it
can be seen front-facing.

Flower: 10cm (4in) wide
Flower spike: 25cm (10in) long
Plant: 12cm (5in) high

Paphiopedilum Jac Flash (right)

This is one of the modern breed of very dark-colored hybrids produced by crossing with selected varieties of the species _P. callosum_. This terrestrial species is still grown today, with attractive light and dark green mottled foliage and its purple and green flower on a tall, slender stem. Discovered in 1885, it originates from Thailand and Indochina (now Vietnam), and has produced its own brand of desirable hybrids for over one hundred years. This hybridization has led to some exciting shades very near to the elusive black. The large, flared dorsal sepal is heavily stained purple, with darker veining, while the swept-down petals are green and purple, and the pouch shows the darkest color of all. The compact plants produce attractive mottled foliage, with short, rounded leaves and make good houseplants even when not in bloom. Jac Flash blooms mainly in summer and will last for several weeks.

Flower: 5cm (2in) wide
Flower spike: 25cm (10in) long
Plant: 10cm (4in) high

**Phragmipedium besseae,
(left) found growing on
inaccessible rock faces
high in the Andes, has
given rise to numerous
red and orange hybrids.**

phragmipediums

Of the three genera discussed that make up the slipper orchids, *Phragmipedium* is the smallest group. But although it contains the least species, these are highly collectible and excite great interest. Phragmipediums are usually terrestrial, although a few can grow as epiphytes on river banks or rocky cliff faces overhanging water. In these situations, the plants cope with the daily downpours or thunderstorms that continually drench them. Because they grow in a well-draining site, with water moving through the roots very fast, the constant wetting is not a problem—a point to remember when watering these orchids at home.

Bearing some resemblance to the paphiopedilums, these plants are usually more tufted and vigorous in growth, producing strap-like leaves from 10cm (4in) to 1m (3ft) long. Their tall flower spikes are sequential blooming so that within a few days of the first flower dropping off, a second and third will replace it, to continue in this way for months. It is normal for one flower spike to keep producing blooms for eighteen months to two years. While a few species bear rounded flowers, similar to paphiopedilums, with the typical pouch, the flowers are mostly large and spiky, with long, narrow, pointed petals that droop impressively to suggest their common name, "mandarin orchids." These eye-catching blooms, up to 15cm (6in) across, are found in a blend of pastel greens and leafy browns, while the smaller, rounded blooms can be a pretty shell pink; the pink varieties were eagerly sought by the early hybridizers.

Origins

Phragmipedium species are distributed from Guatemala down through the Isthmus of Panama into South America, where they are found growing mostly at high altitudes in the Andean rain forests, but occasionally lower down in the hot, steamy jungles of the Amazon. They came to prominence in the nineteenth century and were cultivated by the early Victorian growers who produced the first hybrids. By the turn of the century, however, all hybridizing stopped and it was another seventy years before further advancements were made with the genus. With only a few species to crossbreed, progress was limited, and since none of the original plants were highly colored, the hybrids were of novelty interest only. It was also found at that time that most of the hybrids were sterile and would not breed on; the early hybridizers had no modern-day knowledge of genetics and chromosome numbers, which define a

Phragmipedium longifolium
(this page)

The dramatic flowers of this wonderful display orchid, with their long, narrow, drooping petals, illustrate why phragmipediums are called "mandarin orchids." This species comes from Costa Rica to Colombia, where it grows in the leaf litter as a terrestrial. It was discovered in 1852. On close inspection, the greenish flowers reveal minute spotting and light striping on the petals and pouch. The green staminodium at the center of the bloom is distinguished by its short fringe of black hairs (see above, in close-up). The plant has tall lush foliage and the extremely long spikes produce many flowers in succession.

Flower: 12cm (5in) wide
Flower spike: 2m (6ft) long
Plant: 60cm (24in) high
Pot size: 20cm (8in)

plant's breeding qualities. The situation remained unchanged until the 1980s, when the only phragmipediums in cultivation were wild-collected species, or the survivors from old established stock plants that had been propagated many times. These older plants were rarely good specimens having, over the years, become infected with viruses, but they endured because better plants were unobtainable.

In the 1980s a new species was discovered in Ecuador, causing the orchid sensation of the century and creating a complete revival of the genus. The plant was smaller than most other species, with green foliage and fairly long internodes between the growths, suggesting it grew in competition with many other plants found in the most inaccessible mountain refuges. The collection of these plants was fraught with difficulty, and in places they were reached only by helicopter. The unique red species, named *Phragmipedium besseae* after Libby Besse who found the first plants, soon proved its worth by giving good fertile seed when self-pollinated and passing on to its progeny the ability to grow well and flower easily. Recent hybridizing has produced some wonderfully colored varieties, including pinks, vibrant reds, and fiery oranges.

Cultivation

Phragmipediums thrive in various potting media but the most successful is the inert man made fiber, rockwool, which allows the plants to be kept wetter through the year with no danger of rotting, as with organic potting materials. Fertilizer must be applied regularly to encourage a steady rate of growth for these lush plants, which can even be stood in a tray of water to ensure their roots are continually wet—which would spell instant death to any other orchid! Apart from liking wet conditions at the roots, phragmipediums can be grown in the same way as paphiopedilums (see page 141), in a warm, well-shaded greenhouse with year-round care and the same minimum temperature.

Phragmipedium Grouville (above)
Similar breeding lines can reveal surprises in the range of colors produced, as with this light pink variation among red-flowered hybrids. Grouville's flowers exhibit the familiar classic shape but with pastel rather than rich red hues. One generation on from Eric Young (see page 153), the flower shape reflects the continuing influence of *P. besseae*, which more usually imparts the red coloring to its hybrids. With further buds extending the flower spike, the plant will remain in flower for months before the last flower drops. These lovely bright hybrids still hold novelty value for the collector and amateur grower, but they have a great future ahead.

Flower: 8cm (3in) wide
Flower spike: 30cm (12in)
Plant: 20cm (8in) high

Phragmipedium Sedenii (left)
This beautiful early primary hybrid, raised in 1873 by Veitch & Sons, has stood the test of time and is still available today, though only as a rare collectors' item. The parents are *P. longifolium* and *P. schlimii*, and it was produced when raising orchids from seed was difficult, so only a few plants survived to flowering.

The flowers resemble those of *P. schlimii*, with their pastel coloring typical of older hybrids and in contrast to the bright colors of modern varieties. The tall flower spike carries several buds, not all of which will open at once.

Flower: 6cm (2$^{1}/_{2}$in) wide
Flower spike: 45cm (18in) long
Plant: 30cm (12in) high

Phragmipedium besseae (above)

Until this species was discovered in the 1980s, red coloring was unknown in the genus. It has single-handedly been responsible for opening up a new line of highly desirable plants that are free flowering and easy to grow. Its discovery so late was due in part to the plant's habit of growing on inaccessible rock faces in its native home high in the Andes in Ecuador and Peru. Much sought after by collectors today, the species has given rise to numerous vibrant red and orange hybrids, the like of which was unthinkable a few years ago. The plant produces tufted growths along a creeping rhizome and blooms mainly in the fall, producing its small flowers in succession on a long spike. The oval petals and sides of the pouch have clear, almost transparent sections, but the flower's most notable feature is its brilliant pelargonium red color.

Flower: 8cm (3in) wide
Flower spike: 30cm (12in) long
Plant: 25cm (10in) high
Pot size: 15cm (6in)

Phragmipedium Beauport (below)

This hybrid was raised in 1997 at the Eric Young Orchid Foundation in the Channel Islands, using the light green-flowered Brazilian species *P. sargentianum*, introduced in 1892, and the red-flowered hybrid from *P. besseae*, Hanne Popow. Rounded petals and an egg-shaped pouch set the hybrid apart, combined with its deep, rosy red coloring. The small dorsal sepal is similarly colored, and the flowers are produced in succession on an extending upright flower spike that may not require tying. The plant blooms in late spring from the previous season's growth. While these orchids will divide when there are sufficient growths to one plant, if left to reach specimen size they will produce more than one flower spike at a time, giving a more impressive show of blooms.

Flower: 8cm (3in) wide
Flower spike: 30cm (12in) long
Plant: 20cm (8in) high
Pot size: 12cm (5in)

Phragmipedium Saint Ouen (above)

Another extremely desirable hybrid raised along similar lines, this gives further variety of shape and color. The deep pink has come from the parent *P. besseae*, which also shows in the rigidly held, broad pointed petals. The pouch is prettily striped with a prominent yellow staminodium at the center. The other parent is Hanne Popow, a *P. besseae* hybrid, representing the main line from which we expect the finest varieties in this range. As each flower ages, it drops from the stem while another takes its place, as can be seen on the lower stem, in the illustration above. In this way, the plant will remain in bloom for months on end, making this genus probably the longest-lived in its flowering season.

Flower: 8cm (3in) wide
Flower spike: 30cm (12in) long
Plant: 20cm (8in) high
Pot size: 12cm (5in)

Phragmipedium Saint Peter (above)
The "Saints" series all come from the Eric
Young Orchid Foundation in the Channel
Islands, whose fame has spread worldwide.
Saint Peter is a further variation on the theme
of red-flowered hybrids; its parents are Eric
Young (see page 153), a primary cross
between species *P. longifolium* and *P. besseae*
raised in 1991, and the species *P. longifolium*
(see page 147) itself, which therefore occurs
twice in two generations of this delightful

hybrid. The flower spikes are tall and gracious
and need plenty of headroom if they are to be
grown well. This long-petaled variety carries
a more open pouch, which is a distinctive
feature of the flower.

Flower: 12cm (5in) wide
Flower spike: 45cm (18in) long
Plant: 30cm (12in) high
Pot size: 15cm (6in)

Phragmipedium Corbière (below & right)
Among the latest *Phragmipedium* hybrids are
those produced from the long petaled species.
Their main feature shows up well in this
desirable hybrid, crossing the well-tested
flame-colored Eric Young with an older, long-
petaled primary hybrid, Calurum. Several
long-lasting, light red blooms are produced on
a tall flower spike. The close-up (right) clearly
shows the intriguing formation of the pouch, or
slipper. The leaves are long and straplike, and
the plant needs plenty of space to grow well.
Since its introduction in 1996, this modern
flower has gained worldwide popularity.

Flower: 10cm (4in) wide
Flower spike: 60cm (24in) long
Plant: 45cm (18in) high
Pot size: 20cm (8in)

Phragmipedium Eric Young (below)
This distinctively shaped flower positively
glows with warm orange tones, while its long,
semidrooping petals sweep down from the
horizontal, half-encircling the pouch. To date,
this is one of the finest of the new hybrids
achieved through the introduction of the
magnificent _P. besseae_, which readily imparts
its unique red coloring to its progeny; the
other parent is _P. longifolium_. The hybrid was
raised in 1991, and since has gone on
to produce further generations. The large
flowers are not heavily textured and are easily
supported on the upright flower spike. The
small dorsal sepal is another feature of this
line of breeding.

Flower: 12cm (5in) wide
Flower spike: 45cm (18in) long
Plant: 30cm (12in) high
Pot size: 15cm (6in)

Phragmipedium Don Wimber (above)
In this exciting, richly colored modern hybrid,
the flower is distinctly triangular in shape,
complemented by a well-balanced pouch.
It was raised in Jersey in 1995 from parent
plant Eric Young (see left), crossed back onto
P. besseae to retain the best of the coloring
that distinguishes this group. The flowers
appear on a tall spike, which produces further
buds from the apex as it extends. The plant is
a strong, robust grower with long, straplike
leaves of medium green. These orchids like to
be kept well watered throughout the year so
their fleshy leaves do not become dehydrated
or limp. Light spraying is beneficial, provided
water does not lodge inside the growths.

Flower: 10cm (4in) wide
Flower spike: 60cm (24in) long
Plant: 45cm (18in) high
Pot size: 20cm (8in)

epidendrums

Until it became apparent that there were many separate genera, the first orchids to be recognized and classified all went under the name *Epidendrum*, which means simply "upon a tree" and referred to the orchids' epiphytic habit of attaching themselves to trees as an anchor upon which to grow. Among the epidendrums grown today are the first known tropical orchids, discovered over 200 years ago.

Those orchids remaining in the genus *Epidendrum* are extremely interesting and colorful plants, distributed throughout tropical America; they are mainly tall-growing, with slender, reed-like canes and foliage. The flowers come from the top of the growth and there may be from a few to hundreds, one inflorescence producing successive blooms over many months. The blooms are quite small, seldom more than 2cm (1in) across, but often make up for their lack of size in quantity. Varieties like the red-flowered *E. radicans* become perpetually blooming on a specimen plant, which can reach 1.5m (5ft). They are most at home in tropical gardens, where they grow large, their colors ranging from yellow, orange, and red to green, brown, white, or pink.

Plant the tall-growing species in a bed at one end of an intermediate greenhouse, where there is enough headroom, in a mixture of bark chips or peat and charcoal. As the plants grow, they make copious aerial roots and self-propagate readily from the apex of old stems. Repotting or rebedding is needed only if the plant outgrows its site—otherwise propagations can just be removed and repotted. A smaller group of epidendrums produce the familiar pseudobulbs, tall and slender, with a pair of rigid, long, and oval leaves. The flowers, which come from the apex of the pseudobulbs, are mostly green with narrow petals and sepals dominated by a white three-lobed lip, sometimes frilled along its edge, as in *E. ciliare*. Watering and regular spraying, fertilizing at every third watering, is all these fascinating orchids need to keep them in good health.

***Epidendrum* Plastic Doll** (above)
Looking at the flower shape and coloration of this unusual hybrid, bred in Japan in 1989, it becomes obvious that one parent is the bright *E. pseudepidendrum* (see opposite). There is a close resemblance both in its flowers, especially the protruding lip, and its habit; the other parent is *E. ilense*. Plastic Doll blooms over a long period in summer, after which it rests and needs less water. Leaves are shed a few at a time from the older canes, which become leafless before they shrivel and die. The plants do best in small pots, but need a supporting cane.

Flower: 5cm (2in) wide
Plant: 30-100cm (12-40in) high
Pot size: 15cm (6in)

Epidendrum pseudepidendrum

(this page)

The epidendrums are a genus of many tall-growing plants with thin, leafy canes, or with slender, one-leafed pseudobulbs which resemble cattleyas. Species from the latter group have been crossed with cattleyas to produce the bigeneric hybrid genus of *Epicattleya*, among others. *E. pseudepidendrum* belongs to the reed-type epidendrums, as the other group is known, which contain some extremely interesting orchids that exhibit strange formations and colorings. This species comes from Costa Rica where it grows on trees as an epiphyte, producing extensive stems that bloom from the apex when growth is completed. Several flowers are produced on an arching stem, a combination of bright green, narrowly long sepals and petals with a contrasting glossy orange lip, which is waxy and almost plastic in appearance.

Flower: 5cm (2in) wide
Plant: 30-100cm ((12-40in) high
Pot size: 18cm (7in)

Epidendrum Pink Cascade (above)

Among the tall-growing, reed-type epidendrums there has been only limited hybridizing, often with disappointing results since little advancement is seen to be made. This hybrid is an exception, however, and has proved to be a delightful addition to their numbers. The parents of this British-bred primary hybrid are _E. ilense_ (see opposite) and _E. revolutum;_ it was raised in 1990 by Burnham Nurseries in Devon, England. The plants are not so tall as to be difficult to accommodate within the home, and they bloom on young stems, leafed throughout their length. Numerous pink flowers with rigid, outstretched petals are produced on an arching stem, which is an extension of the leafy growth, and more blooms appear over a period of time, extending the flowering season. The prettily marked blooms are also individually long-lasting.

Flower: 5cm (2in) wide
Plant: 60cm (24in) high
Pot size: 15cm (6in)

Epidendrum ciliare (above)

Originating in the West Indies and tropical America, this _Epidendrum_ is one of a group of similar species that produce slender pseudobulbs with a solitary leaf, not unlike the growth of many laelias, with which they can be interbred. It was described in 1759, making it one of the earliest-known of the tropical epiphytes. The flowers are produced on a lengthy stem from the top of the latest pseudobulb. Up to eight flowers have long, narrow, light green petals and sepals, with an equally long, deeply lobed white lip, frilled at the edge. This is another manifestation of the bearding that appears on the lips of various orchids, its precise function unknown. The fall-blooming species can be shy to flower if not given sufficient light, particularly toward the end of summer, when the pseudobulbs are maturing.

Flower: 9cm (3$^{1}/_{2}$in) wide
Plant: 30cm (12in) high
Pot size: 15cm (6in)

Epidendrum ilense (below)

This robust, tall-growing species from Central America produces leafy stems that bloom from the apex when growth is complete. A recent introduction, it was discovered during the latter decades of the twentieth century, growing in a small area of Costa Rica. The extraordinary flowers are carried on a slender arching stem and appear in succession over a long period, with three to four blooms out at any one time. Their color is off white; the sepals and petals are small but the lip is strangely bulbous at the center, its edge deeply frilled to give a bearded effect. Old, leafless stems continue to produce blooms over several years. This unusual plant needs a fairly large container to prevent it from getting top-heavy.

Flower: 5cm (2in) wide
Plant: 30–100cm (12—40in) high
Pot size: 18cm (7in)

Epidendrum wallisii (above)

This is one of a group of mainly summer-flowering epidendrums that can be grown where there is sufficient headroom for their tall, leafy stems to extend unhindered. At the apex are these delightful flowers, regally colored with purple-spotted yellow petals and sepals, swept back to emphasize the deeply lobed blue-violet lip. This terrestrial species was discovered in Colombia in 1875 growing at an elevation of 1,500m (5,000ft) by the orchid collector, Gustav Wallis. Originally described as *Epidendrum wallisii*, under which name it is still widely known, it was transferred to its present genus of *Oerstedella* in 1981. While these are vigorous growers, they do not divide or propagate easily, and you must be prepared for the plants to become very large over a period of several years. Only when they have reached specimen size, with several new growths all blooming at the same time, can they be viewed at their full potential.

Flower: 5cm (2in) wide
Plant: 45cm (18in) high
Pot size: 12cm (5in)

coelogynes and other genera

Coelogynes are a genus of mainly cool-growing orchids from the Indian continent and elsewhere (see page 94). But they have also extended their natural range to Malaysia and Borneo, and those that grow at the edge of their natural habitat require more warmth. Among these intermediate coelogynes are some superb evergreen orchids, producing large, oval to cone-shaped pseudobulbs topped by two wide ribbed leaves up to 60cm (24in) long. Their flowering habits vary from those that produce a single bloom in succession on a drooping spike (*C. speciosa*, see below) to those carrying numerous large blooms on a pendent spike below the foliage. The latter group's flowers are prized for their deep apple green coloring, while the fiddle-shaped lip is black-warted, smudged, and veined.

Grow the warmer-loving coelogynes in the greenhouse, where there is enough headroom for their large leaves and where they will have a minimum temperature of 10°C (50°F) and a maximum of 30°C (86°F). They need plenty of water and fertilizer from spring through summer, with light shade overhead. Their new growths will take all season to develop, and when the pseudobulbs have matured, they can rest until new growth starts again. There are few hybrids within this group, and relatively few species, but their startling flowers will brighten spring and early summer. And there are many more orchids, less widely grown, which are suitable for growing indoors, provided they can have extra warmth in winter. *Ludisia*, for example, is a low-light plant growing on river banks in deep shade, while the miniature *Liparis unata* is a terrestrial plant growing in tropical Asia as well as Europe and Britain.

Ludisia discolor (above)
This terrestrial species from China and Southeast Asia is grown as much for its decorative foliage as its flowers. It is one of a number known as "jewel orchids," for the delicate veining, which shows red on the dark velvety green leaves and glistens when lit by the sun. In their natural habitat these plants grow in deep shade and humid conditions in mossy banks along rivers. The plant forms leafy growths along a creeping rhizome. When completed, a flowering stem arises from the center; its intricate white blooms resemble little bees flying. Keep this evergreen species moist all year; it does best on a well-lit windowsill or in a warm greenhouse, without too much humidity around it. It needs a winter temperature of 13°C (55°F) min.

Flower: 1cm ($^1/_2$in) wide
Plant: 10cm (4in) high
Pot size: 12cm (5in)

Coelogyne speciosa (left)
A number of tall-growing *Coelogyne* species are remarkable for their amazing lip markings and coloration. This species from Sumatra exhibits the best qualities of the group: The flowers are large, the sepals light buff or cream, with the slender, hardly visible petals hidden behind the sepals. The lip, covered with ridges and fine hairs, is deep chocolate brown at the center. The plant produces cone-shaped pseudobulbs with two widely oval leaves, and the flower spikes come from the center of the new growth while it is at a young stage. Several blooms are produced, but only one opens at a time, spreading the flowering season over several weeks in late summer. The modest amount of hybridizing that has been done with this species shows little improvement over the species itself.

Flower: 6cm ($2^1/_2$in) wide
Plant: 30cm (12in) high
Pot size: 15cm (6in)

Coelogyne massangeana

(this page)

This tall-growing species makes an impressive plant with large oval pseudobulbs topped by two wide oval leaves. The flower spikes emerge from the young new growth and plunge dramatically over the side of the pot to bloom along its length. Numerous flowers, light buff brown with yellow and brown on the lip, are produced in the spring and last for up to three weeks. The species comes from Malaysia and Borneo where it grows on trees in mountainous regions. It has been cultivated for many years and propagates freely.

Flower: 4cm (1½in) wide
Plant: 60cm (24in) high
Pot size: 25cm (10in)

Coelogyne Green Dragon 'Chelsea' AM/RHS (below)

Among the most easily grown coelogynes are a number from Malaysia that need warmer conditions. They are larger in their growth and produce correspondingly bigger flowers, but where there is enough room for their lush foliage, they offer dramatic color and flowering habits. This unusual hybrid has retained the apple green coloring of one parent species, *C. pandurata*, with the intricate lip markings of the other, *C. massangeana* (see page 159). The flowers are produced theatrically—the spike pushes up and out of the new growth to plunge vertically in an extending chain until the buds swell and open their flowers.

Flower: 5cm (2in) wide
Plant: 60cm (24in) high
Pot size: 25cm (10in)

Zygopetalum maxillare (above)

This is a plant for the collector. The species comes from Brazil where it grows epiphytically, producing its scant pseudobulbs wide apart along a strong, creeping, and upright rhizome. It has several long, narrow medium green leaves, as well as short aerial roots at regular intervals along the stem. The plant is best grown in a pot into which a mossy pole has been inserted, or it may be grown on a stout piece of cork bark with a pad of sphagnum moss tied to it, so that the roots will grow into it and gather moisture. Waxy, fragrant flowers, up to six or eight on a spike, appear in the fall. They are among the most colorful orchids in the genus, which is remarkable for the somber purple and brown coloring characteristic of most other species. The close-up shown here reveals the dark purple coloring that radiates out across the lip, while the light green petals and sepals are heavily overlaid with bronzy brown.

Flower: 5cm (2in) wide
Plant: 90cm (36in) high
Pot size: 15cm (6in)
Temperature: 13°C (55°F) min.,
   30°C (86°F) max.

Liparis unata

(above left)
Many orchids
can be termed
true miniatures, producing intricate little flowers that have a charm of their own. Such a species is *Liparis unata*, belonging to a large, extremely variable genus widely distributed throughout a great portion of the world. Very few are in cultivation, however, due to their being small terrestrial plants with minute blooms. *L. unata* is one of the more colorful and interesting species, a joy to grow and to see in bloom. The exquisite, insectlike flowers have diminutive sepals and petals with a relatively large, richly colored lip. It produces small pseudobulbs along a creeping rhizome with a single wide leaf and remains evergreen all year.

Flower: 1cm (¹/2in) wide
Plant: 15cm (6in) high
Pot size:12cm (5in)
Temperature: 10°C (50°F) min., 30°C (86°F) max.

Aspasia lunata (right)

This is a small-growing, lesser-known member of the *Odontoglossum* alliance, grown for its attraction as a species in its own right. It produces small, lengthened pseudobulbs with a pair of narrow leaves and will quickly establish itself as a specimen if left undivided for a few years. In addition to being grown in a pot, this species can also grow in a hanging basket. Its early-summer flowers are carried on shortened spikes, with a single star-shaped bloom. The narrow petals and sepals are green, speckled with brown, and the flared lip is white, with rosy mauve toward the center. The flowers most closely resemble brassias and will crossbreed with them and related orchids.

Flower: 5cm (2in) wide
Plant: 15cm (6in) high
Pot size: 12cm (5in)
Temperature range 10°C (50°F) min.,
   30°C (86°F) max.

warm-g

Those orchids included in the warm-growing range require temperatures that are higher at night but not necessarily by day. Since they do not need the same variation as cooler-growing orchids, this makes them ideal garden plants in tropical parts of the world, where temperatures fluctuate by only about 7°C (10°F) between day and night, summer and winter. The same orchids also grow well indoors in more temperate climates, where overnight central heating provides minimum background warmth of 18°C (64°F). The year-round daytime temperature can be the same as for cooler-growing orchids in summer, or a little higher. As the temperature range decreases, so does the variety of plants that can be accommodated in the narrower band.

In this group we find the demurely beautiful *Phalaenopsis*, the exquisite "moth orchids," which have become one of today's top indoor orchids. In tropical parts of the world like the West Indies, the outdoor climate is too hot for even these warm-loving plants. Those that really come into their own in the tropics are the vandas and their gloriously colored hybrids, produced for outdoor culture. Lapping up the sun, high humidity, and year-round bright light, these jewels of the East are forever blooming.

rowing

orchids

phalaenopsis

Phalaenopsis have undergone a phenomenal rise in popularity in the last two decades. Among the first of the tropical orchids to gain favor in Victorian collections, the species were cultivated for their attractive flowers on long branching stems, but only a few were considered desirable, and hybridizing with these was slow and unrewarding. For many years, therefore, little or no advancement was made, though the species were commonly sought after.

Horticulturally, the genus *Phalaenopsis* can be loosely divided into two types. There are those with long, often branching spikes and large, softly textured, well-rounded blooms in pastel shades of pink and white. The other group carry their flowers on a shortened spike, producing less rounded, waxy flowers with brighter colorings. Intensive breeding between the two groups has caused them to merge into a great family of superb hybrids, with dazzling colors and variations once thought impossible. This modern hybridizing has revolutionized the genus, carrying it to the pinnacle of success. Within the *Phalaenopsis* alliance is a large number of intergeneric hybrids, the most important of which are *Doritaenopsis* (*Doritis* x *Phalaenopsis*) and *Doricentrum* (*Doritis* x *Ascocentrum*); both bigeneric crosses have heightened color introduced by *Doritis*. *Ascocentrum* is allied to the vandas (*Ascocentrum* x *Vanda* produces *Ascocenda*), but will also interbreed with *Phalaenopsis* and *Doritis* to give different results.

The best *Phalaenopsis* varieties have been extended to include combinations of white petals and sepals with highly decorative lips in red and orange, while the pinks have been developed to encompass the richest shades of purple. Though generally self-colored, the pastel pinks and whites may be overlaid with candy stripes, spotted, or dusted with darker colors. Yellow coloring has also come to the fore, and you can now find pure or spotted yellows, sometimes bordering on lime or gold. The smallest of the yellow hybrids carry numerous flowers, 2cm (1in) across, on spikes under 30cm (12in) tall. For ease of growing and regular flowering, these orchids have no equal, which is why more phalaenopsis are being raised throughout the world today than any other orchid. The species are still grown in specialty collections and individual plants can be found in dedicated orchid nurseries, while the hybrids are available in their thousands from outlets that include florists and nurseries.

Origins

Phalaenopsis come from Malaysia, Borneo, and the islands of the Philippines. Growing naturally in the tree canopy, well protected from the sun above, these epiphytic plants are shade-loving, and their fleshy leaves would quickly burn if subjected to direct sunlight. When viewed at ground level by the early explorers, the flowers appeared to shimmer and dance in the breeze, resembling a swarm of moths and earning them their common name of "moth orchids." The monopodial *Phalaenopsis* have no pseudobulbs but grow from a central rhizome, producing thick, fleshy, dark green, oval leaves, singly. An adult plant carries just four or five leaves at any one time, shedding the older leaves at the rate of about one a year; flower spikes emerge from the base of the latest mature leaf. Their roots are flattened, silvery, and meandering and are often produced outside the pot, where they become aerial and adhere to any surface they contact.

Modern *Phalaenopsis* hybrids do not have a particular flowering period, but produce a flower spike in response to the completion of a new leaf. The larger varieties can have spikes up to a meter (3 feet) tall; these need support to ensure they do not bend under their own weight or get broken accidentally. The compact varieties, with smaller flowers, are ideally suited to growing indoors. *Phalaenopsis* flowers last for many weeks in perfection, and when the last bloom has faded and dropped from the stem, this can be cut back to a lower node, so that within a few weeks a secondary flowering stem will grow from below the cut to prolong the flowering. A single mature plant can remain in bloom indefinitely, as new flower spikes replace the older ones before they have finished, so that with just a small selection of plants, you can achieve flowers all year round.

Light striping over a pale base contrasts with the cherry-red lip in the popular, well-shaped hybrid, Miss Print (left).

Cultivation

Phalaenopsis grow steadily throughout the year, slowing down during winter in response to shorter daylight hours and lower temperatures and speeding up in spring and summer. Their seasons are less marked than in other orchids, making them easier to handle as houseplants; they also adapt more readily to drier conditions. Indoors they are quite happy in a position of semi-shade, well away from direct sunlight but in a warm spot where there is little fluctuation between day and night, summer and winter temperatures. The plants grow equally well in a warm greenhouse, with a minimum winter night temperature of 18°C (64°F), rising in the day by at least 7°C (10°F), while in summer temperatures as high as 30°C (86°F) will not harm them.

Lightly spray or mist *Phalaenopsis* leaves in summer, but keep water out of the center, where it will cause rotting if left. Discontinue spraying in winter, when the water can remain for too long on the leaf surface. Plants growing indoors may be regularly sponged over to keep the leaves free from dust. Few pests attack *Phalaenopsis*, although aphids may congregate on the developing flower spikes and buds, and false red spider mite can affect the leaves (see page 217). The most vulnerable part of the plant is the center crown from which the new leaves emerge. Rot caused by cold or wet conditions can start here, usually in winter when the plants are more at risk. In this case, the center leaf will pull away and be brown and wet at the base. Once the center has rotted, the plant often attempts to grow again from near the base, producing a healthy new plant by the side of the original; the leaves on the older plant eventually turn yellow and drop off. If no new growth appears within six weeks, however, the plant is likely to die.

Repot *Phalaenopsis* in spring or fall, when they are not in flower; leave any aerial roots outside the container, trimming them back if damaged. As *Phalaenopsis* do not make extensive roots within the pot, you can often return them to the same size container once all dead roots have been removed; unless otherwise stated, a 12cm (5in) pot is most suitable. In their natural state, some species grow downward, their long leaves becoming pendant and hanging free; this assists drainage and prevents the center of the plant from filling with water. In cultivation many hybrids attempt to grow likewise but, for ease of handling, place them upright when repotting and support the plant with a short cane.

Long sprays of pure yellow flowers ensure that hybrids like Yellow Treasure (above left) remain a lovely alternative to the pink and white varieties of *Phalaenopsis*. See page 173 for a full entry.

A close-up of *Phalaenopsis* Golden Bells (left) shows the lip detail and the yellow-patterned base coloring of the petals. See page 168 for a full entry.

Phalaenopsis Sweet Memory (above)
A further dimension has been created by the introduction of breeding from the species, *P. violacea*, which has here been crossed with an older primary hybrid, Deventeriana (1927). While *P. violacea* has dominated the texture, shape, and lip of this hybrid, the rich coloring comes from Deventeriana. The individual flowers are richly colored, with darker overtones on a light base, which contrasts with the deep red of the lip. The blooms have a heavier texture and a more open shape than more conventional hybrids. These plants can become considerably large-leafed, producing tall, branching flower spikes to give a wonderful show; summer appears to be their peak flowering period. The original cross has been remade for modern breeding purposes, and Sweet Memory is typical of the exciting hybrids within this group.

Flower: 8cm (3in) wide
Flower spike: 60cm (24in) long
Plant: 38cm (15in) high
Pot size: 15cm (6in)

Phalaenopsis Golden Bells (below)
This very pretty variety has distinct deep yellow dotting over a pale yellow ground, which gives a pleasing, unusual combination The russet-red highlight at the center of the white lip gives the whole flower a bright appearance. Golden Bells has the well-known yellow Golden Sands as one parent, while the other, the species *P. venosa*, has shortened the flowering spikes. The yellow varieties produce slightly smaller flowers that keep their color throughout the long flowering period, and the more compact flower spike will remain upright without the need for a supporting cane, making this an ideal plant to grow where space is limited.

Flower: 6cm (2^{1}/$_{2}$in) wide
Flower spike: 25cm (10in) long
Plant: 20cm (8in) high
Pot size: 10cm (4in)

Phalaenopsis Paifang's Golden Lion (right)
Heavy leopard spotting overlies this lighter-based flower, giving the impression of deep rosy purple. The lateral petals are neatly divided along the center vein, below which the color becomes intensified. Such exquisite coloring is found only in this type of hybrid, which produces glossy, waxy-textured flowers in a perfectly symmetrical shape on a shorter stem; the individual flowers, produced in succession, remain a long time in bloom. As mature flowers fade, new buds are continually opening along an extending stem. Paifang's Golden Queen is the mother plant of the selective breeding line that has produced many superb spotted varieties from a pink form of the variable species, *P. lueddemanniana*. This hybrid was raised in 1992 by Paifang's Orchid Garden in Taiwan.

Flower: 8cm (3in) wide
Flower spike: 23cm (9in) long
Plant: 20cm (8in) high
Pot size: 10cm (4in)

Phalaenopsis Follett (below)
In this luscious hybrid, the petal decoration of delicate veining and stripes has been taken to its full potential and the perfectly shaped flowers are enhanced by the deeper lip. This Californian-bred hybrid, raised in 1993, is the result of a long line of specialized breeding from Doris, an important breeding plant of its day, raised in 1940. The hybrid has come so far that it bears little resemblance to the original tall-flowered Filipino species. The popular, beautifully decorative orchids are often sold under the name "candy stripes." Well-grown, mature plants of candy-striped varieties produce long, branching flower spikes with blooms that open from the lowest on a stem to the buds at the end in less than a week.

Flower: 8cm (3in) wide
Flower spike: 75cm (30in) long
Plant: 30cm (12in) high

Phalaenopsis Hawaiian Darling (above)
This delightful modern hybrid was raised in Hawaii, where many new strains are now emerging. It is the result of back-crossing the large, pink-flowered hybrid Lippegruss, of German origin, with the delicate, showy P. stuartiana, from the Philippines. This species carries many flowers on a tall spike, the blooms white with brown leopard spotting on the lateral sepals and lip. In this new hybrid, the marking has come through as rosy mauve spotting on the lower sepals, which are partially hidden by the well-rounded petals. The basically white flower has a slight pink flush retained from the pink hybrid parent. Another desirable quality is the arching habit of the spike, which naturally arranges the blooms in a descending spray. The plant will bloom two to three times a year, the long-lasting flowers remaining for several weeks.

Flower: 6cm (2¹/₂in) wide
Flower spike: 75cm (30in) tall
Plant: 10cm (4in) high
Pot size: 10cm (4in)

Phalaenopsis San Luca (above)

The rich red coloring of this fine modern hybrid is uncommon and has been achieved only by the dedication of the hybridizers, in this instance in California, where young plants can be brought to flowering size in the shortest possible time. Similar breeding through successive generations, as in Follett, has produced a combination of the splash-petal effect behind the candy-striped veining, offset by the ruby red lip. The large blooms are produced on the end of tall flower spikes with several nodes along their length. When the initial flowering has finished, further branches of flowers can be activated by cutting the end of the stem back to a lower node. While this can be done with almost any *Phalaenopsis*, it is most successful with the long-stemmed varieties. Secondary flowerings produce smaller flowers, however, and they must not be encouraged at the expense of a plant that is to be grown on for a number of years, since excessive flowering will only weaken it.

Flower: 9cm (3^1/$_2$in) wide
Flower spike: 75cm (30in) long
Plant: 30cm (12in) high

Phalaenopsis Brother Buddha (above)
The Brother hybrids are the result of a huge
wave of hybridizing in Taiwan, this one a
cross between Fortune Buddha and Brother
Angel, raised in 1992 by Brothers Orchid
Nursery. The yellow-flowered varieties
generally produce slightly smaller flowers but
their reduced size is more than made up for
by the lovely coloring and patterning that
overlays many of this type. The plants are
more compact and the flower spikes shorter
with, usually, fewer flowers on a spike. The
blooms are neatly placed on the stem and
displayed horizontally, rather than drooping
on long arching or pendent spikes, as seen in
the white, pink, and newer red varieties.
Once the flowers begin to age, they lose a
little of their brightness and tone down to
a paler shade. Individual blooms often look
almost transparent before falling from the stem.

Flower: 6cm (2^1/$_2$ in) wide
Flower spike: 25cm (10in) long
Plant: 30cm (12in) high

Phalaenopsis Yellow Treasure (below)
Yellow Treasure is an example of the lovely,
clear yellow varieties available to those who
prefer flowers that are plain and simple.
It is one of the latest yellow hybrids to come
from the Pacific Rim, where the expanding
nurseries are now exporting to a worldwide
market. Yellow-flowered _Phalaenopsis_ vary
from almost-white flowers, with pale yellow
radiating out from the center, to the deep,
self-colored hybrids, which take on an almost
golden tinge. They contrast sharply with lime-
colored flowers, which can look cool on the
hottest day.

Flower: 8cm (3in) wide
Flower spike: 30cm (12in) long
Plant: 30cm (12in) high

Phalaenopsis Culiacan (right)
A flower with pearl-white sepals
and petals and a clean yellow lip
makes a beautiful contrast. This
flower's appearance is perhaps
close to the original species that so
captivated the early explorers
when they hunted these exotic
blooms in the topmost branches
of giant trees in the forests of the
Philippine Islands. This French-bred
hybrid is the latest in a long line of
thoroughbreds that have been kept
pure of color. Its parents are Gatto
and Fairy Tales, raised in 1992 by
Zuma Canyon of California.
The breeding goes back many generations
to Cassandra, a stepping-stone parent and
primary hybrid raised by Veitch in 1896
from _P. equestris_ and _P. stuartiana_.

Flower: 9cm (3¹/₂in) wide
Flower spike: 75cm (30in) long
Plant: 30cm (12in) high

The branching sprays of
Phalaenopsis flowers dancing in
the wind drew the attention of
hunters who, from a distance,
could not make out whether they
were looking at a swarm of moths
or a cluster of exotic flowers.

Phalaenopsis Pink Twilight (left)

This appealing flower is typical of the pink-flowered varieties raised using successive generations of pink Filipino species, such as, in this case, *P. schilleriana* and *P. sanderiana*. Pink Twilight has large, showy blooms, with the flowers arranged neatly along two sides of the stem. The stem assumes an arching habit under its own weight as the flowers open; these blooms can be produced at various times of the year and last for many weeks. The intricate detail of the lip is shown enlarged to reveal the minute decoration and rather mysterious shape, that spells out a direct message to the pollinating insect. Hybridizing has greatly enhanced the lip decoration to match our idea of what is attractive. Many different varieties can be found in this color range, all of which will produce flowers two or three times a year.

Flower: 8cm (3in) wide
Flower spike: 30cm (12in) long
Plant: 30cm (12in) high

Phalaenopsis Romantic Tango (below)

Having produced numerous hybrids among the clear white and pretty pink types, the challenge for breeders was to move on to a semi-alba flower with white or pale pink petals and sepals, and to combine the pastel coloring with a rich, darker-colored lip. This modern French-bred hybrid is the latest in a long line of such color variants; its parents are Culiba and Boutique, a Dutch hybrid raised in 1994. The influence of natural hybrid *P. x intermedia* gives the large, ruby-red lip. The flowers are produced on long sprays; their petals overlap each other. These varieties will bloom at any time, on tall spikes, and their coloring can vary according to the season. The color of flowers produced in spring and summer, when the light is brighter, will be more intense than those produced in winter.

Flower: 8cm (3in) wide
Flower spike: 45cm (18in) long
Plant: 30cm (12in) high

Phalaenopsis Fajen's Fireworks (above)

Hybrids produced in one part of the world will often run alongside similar developments in other countries, as all breeders of fine orchids are looking for similar attributes. This example shows a line of breeding popular in France, where plants grown under a particular set of climatic conditions are produced for a world market, which means they may finish up growing in any country, often far from that of their raising. Such is the versatility of these vigorous plants that they will grow in any situation where they are kept warm and comfortable, and their few requirements are met. Fajen's Fireworks is produced by the Florida nursery, Fajen's Orchids and Exotics, which has used the same line of breeding, starting with the species *P. stuartiana* and *P. x intermedia*, to produce this particular hybrid from Dame de Coeur and Kathleen Ai in 1991. The combination of line veining throughout the petals, breaking up into delicate spotting on the lower sepals, form the perfect backdrop to the intensified lip color that is this hybrid's main feature.

Flower: 8cm (3in) wide
Flower spike: 45cm (18in) long
Plant: 30cm (12in) high

Phalaenopsis Lipperose (above)
This delicately colored German-bred hybrid is a winner. It was raised in 1968 from Ruby Wells and Zade and represents a long line of quality pink-flowered varieties that have become popular around the world. In its day it was ahead of its time, producing the first of the large pink flowers and regarded as a breakthrough in the breeding of quality phalaenopsis, previously led by the whites. The soft hues have been retained from the original species. A well-grown plant that misses a flowering can sometimes be encouraged to bloom by lowering the minimum temperature for a few weeks, which will almost certainly initiate the flower spike into activity.

Flower: 8cm (3in) wide
Flower spike: 30cm (12in) long
Plant: 30cm (12in) high

Phalaenopsis **Little Skipper** (right)

A pretty group known as the Little Guys, these miniature varieties produce numerous flowers on compact plants and can be relied on to bloom several times during the year. On occasion they may become almost perpetually blooming, with new flower spikes being produced before the last one has lost its blooms. The main colorings within this small group are pink or pink and white, with deeper red lips in harmony with the rest of the flower. The gracefully arching flower spikes become pendent if unsupported, and their main flowering peaks during the fall and winter. Little Skipper is a 1991 hybrid from California, one of a new line of breeding that may still have much to show us in future generations.

Flower: 5cm (2in) wide
Flower spike: 23cm (9in) long
Plant: 15cm (6in) high
Pot size: 10cm (4in)

Phalaenopsis **Petite Snow** (below left)

Selective breeding from the smaller species within the genus has resulted in a much reduced flower, produced in quantity on a compact flower spike. Petite Snow is an offspring of the much-used breeding parent, Cassandra. Crossed back onto the species *P. stuartiana* in 1985 by Richella in Hawaii, it has itself gone on to produce further notable hybrids of the smaller type. This little gem combines the qualities of the larger types in cheerful rosy pink colorings and is ideal where space is more limited, or when the collection becomes larger as more plants are added. The flowers open all together on the spike, which arches naturally and needs little support. It is not unusual for this type to produce more than one flower spike at a time, giving an excellent show of blooms for its size.

Flower: 5cm (2in) wide
Flower spike: 23cm (9in) long
Plant: 15cm (6in) high
Pot size: 10cm (4in)

Phalaenopsis **Hisa Lady Rose** (above)

Hisa Lady Rose, a cross from Otohime and Paradise Glow, was raised in 1988 in Japan and is the latest in a long line of Japanese-bred plants, using the well-known Doris and its offspring Zada as starting points. These parent plants are American- and German-bred hybrids respectively, making the new lines truly global. *Phalaenopsis* are among the most rewarding orchids for the beginner to grow because of their willingness to grow and flower in conditions that are found in most homes. Treated with care, the plants will live for many years without becoming too large or difficult to handle. Their size is self-regulating as the older leaves are shed to make way for the formation of new ones from the center of the plant.

Flower: 9cm (3^1/2in) wide
Flower spike: 75cm (30in) long
Plant: 30cm (12in) high

Doritis pulcherrima 'Chumpenensis'
(below)

A smaller relative of *Phalaenopsis*, this delightful and unique clone of the species is becoming popular in its own right, as well as for the hybrids raised from it. Originally discovered in 1833 in Vietnam, the pretty *D. pulcherrima* is one of only three species in the genus; it is highly variable and several color forms are known. *Doritis* will breed with *Phalaenopsis* to give the bigeneric genus, *Doritaenopsis*, producing vertical flower spikes whose small prettily colored blooms open in succession until the whole spike is in full flower. 'Chumpenensis' is an unusual clone of a species that is normally rose-purple or lilac-purple in color. Its flowers show an unusual mutation where the yellow lip markings are repeated on the petals. The blooms appear at any time of year and last for several weeks.

Flower: 2cm (1in) wide
Flower spike: 30cm (12in) long
Plant: 15cm (6in) high
Pot size: 10cm (4in)

Doritaenopsis Quevedo (above)

This extremely pretty hybrid has originated from California and is one of a cluster of varieties raised from smaller-flowered species, such as *P. equestris*, which has numerous pink flowers on a short spike. This species was crossed with the larger white-flowered species *P. stuartiana* to produce the primary hybrid, Cassandra, which became a popular breeding plant. Two generations on and with the input of the white-flowered *Doritis pulcherrima* var. *alba*, this lovely white-flowered bigeneric hybrid has appeared. The freely branching spike has come from the *P. equestris* ancestor, whose shape is slightly discernible in the long lip. This hybrid gives a fantastic show of bloom on a compact plant, with its pleasing contrast of white petals and cherry-red lip.

Flower: 5cm (2in) wide
Flower spike: 75cm (30in) long
Plant: 10cm (4in) high
Pot size: 10cm (4in)

***Doritaenopsis* Pinlong Gleam** (above)
This hybrid, raised in 1982 by a Taiwan
nursery, is the product of a crossing between
Phalaenopsis and *Doritis*. Several instances of
Doritis pulcherrima arise in its pedigree, with
different clones being used. Also in the
background appear Doris and Zada, the
same hybrids giving a variety of results when
used in different combinations. These flowers
have a more open, starry appearance with an
intensity of color seldom found in the pure
Phalaenopsis. Small flowers are produced on
an upright flower spike, the petals and sepals
slightly concave along their length.

Flower: 8cm (3in) wide
Flower spike: 30cm (12in) long
Plant: 30cm (12in)

Phalaenopsis readily
interbreed with
other related genera,
and in recent years
more intergeneric
hybrids have
appeared, some with
startling results,
creating an ever-
wider range of
superb hybrids.

***Doricentrum* Pulcherrimum** (below)
By crossing *Doritis* with *Ascocentrum*, a further
breeding line opens up to give highly colored
flowers of a distinct shape and a great deal of
character. This *Doricentrum* hybrid was
registered in 1969 and, more recently, a
cross between *D. pulcherrima* and *A. miniatum*
was raised in Florida, but very few others
have appeared in this bigeneric genus.
The distinctive sepals and petals are flat and
held rigidly outward, while the lip has its own
unique shape, inherited from the *Ascocentrum*
parent. These dainty blooms are carried on
an upright flower spike that is self-supporting.
Though the flowers can appear at almost any
time, summer is the peak season. Since this
type of breeding is relatively new, such
varieties are most likely to be found in specialty
nurseries, where their bright colors and lovely
flowers ensure they are in great demand.

Flower: 1cm (^{1}/2in) wide
Flower spike: 15cm (6in) long
Plant: 10cm (4in) high
Pot size: 10cm (4in)

the vanda alliance

Vandas produce the most gorgeous, huge, brightly colored blooms and would undoubtedly be grown in every home and greenhouse if the plants were as easy to accommodate as they are beautiful. Their gaudy colors reflect the tropical climate and year-round sunshine with which their cultivation is synonymous. They readily interbreed with closely related genera, including *Eulanthe*, *Ascocentrum*, and others, to produce the multitude of coveted hybrids grown today. All are monopodial orchids, producing pairs of long semirigid leaves from an upright, ever-growing rhizome. The plants can grow tall, up to a meter (3 feet), with long, stiffened aerial roots descending well below it. Though evergreen, they lose their foliage occasionally, one or two leaves at a time. The flower spikes appear from the base of a lower leaf and grow speedily to produce up to twelve, more usually about six, large flamboyant flowers, varying in size from 5–15cm (2–6in). Their glamorous rounded petals overlap the sepals, while the much smaller lip is insignificant by comparison. They bloom at various times, with peak flowering in spring and early summer.

Unusually among orchids, vandas' most prominent color is blue, which may be pale sky to deep violet, the coloring mottled or tessellated over a lighter tone. Other colors include mauves and purples, and breeding with related genera has produced vibrant reds, fiery oranges, and yellows bordering on green, with all hues in between. But it is the coveted blue for which these admirable orchids are best known.

Origins

Vandas are natives of India and Myanmar, and are also found in Malaysia and the islands of Borneo and the Philippines, where they grow as epiphytes, often in full sun. While not a large genus, hybridizing from the earliest times has created a flamboyant range of rainbow colors. The first hybrids were made in Europe from imported species, but today these orchids are raised in their thousands in the tropical countries where they grow and flower with ease. The main specialty nurseries are in Thailand and Florida, where the plants are grown under shade cloths, which provide the minimum of protection from the sun. Here they revel in warmth and moisture, their abundant flowering triggered by the tropical sunshine. They grow fast, alternating their new leaves from left to right to produce a large, handsome, fan-shaped plant.

Cut flowers, such as this *Vanda* Memoria Lyle Swanson 'Justin Grannel' (left), can be flown around the world in water tubes, to ensure the orchids remain fresh. See page 185 for a full entry.

A close-up of *Vanda* Violeta 'Fuchs Sky' (right) shows the small lip, typical of the genus and used as a platform by alighting insects. See page 185 for a full entry.

Cultivation

Outside of the tropics, vandas do not make good houseplants and will only be found in specialty nurseries where a limited selection may be offered. Their cultivation indoors often leads to disappointment where the drier atmosphere and inaccessibility to year-long light inhibits their growth, and where they are prone to rapid dehydration. But in a warm greenhouse with a sunny spot, vandas can be tried by enthusiastic growers willing to rise to the challenge of growing these demanding, but very rewarding, orchids. Some vandas are more adaptable than others and the fabled *Vanda* Rothschildiana, with its huge blue flowers, and its hybrids are the outstanding exception. They can be grown and flowered with comparable ease, even in the less sunny climates of Britain and parts of Europe. This *Vanda* is a primary hybrid first raised in 1931, since when the cross has been repeated many times. On one side is *Vanda coerulea*, a soft, sky-blue-flowered plant growing high in the Himalayas, where cold nights are normal through part of the year, while the other parent is *Vanda* (*Eulanthe*) *sanderiana*, a warm-growing species native to the Philippines. The resulting cross has created a plant with an unusually wide temperature tolerance,

This unusual trigeneric hybrid, *Christieara* Renée Gerber 'Fuchs Confetti' (below), produces distinctive flowers on dense, upright spikes. See page 191 for a full entry.

enabling it to be grown the world over.

In summer, vandas do best with full sun and high humidity in a greenhouse where the temperature does not drop below 16–18°C (60–65°F) at night. During the day this can rise safely to 30°C (86°F), with a significant increase in humidity to match the tropical environment they prefer as nearly as possible. These

The twisted stems of *Ascocenda* Fuchs Sunkist 'Mike' (above) show how the flowers turn before opening to a position where their lips are displayed horizontally. See page 190 for a full entry.

temperatures should be adhered to closely, even in winter. Grown well, the plants will flower several times a year, but this reward may prove elusive. Vandas may be grown conventionally in pots or, better still, in open, slatted wooden baskets. Fill the basket with chunky pieces of bark and horticultural charcoal, a mix that is usually firm enough to support the plant and hold it in the container. Ideally, hang the baskets near to the glass in the greenhouse roof, where it is also warmer in winter. This mode of growing allows the long aerial roots to extend downward, where they can grow to over a meter (3 feet) long. Watering is best done by regular, twice-daily spraying, misting the entire plant and its roots. As the temperature falls toward evening, the humidity will rise naturally, benefiting the plants, which need not be sprayed again until the next morning, to allow time for any water lodging in the top axil to dry out; this part is vulnerable to rot. If it becomes too wet, new growth will be made from lower down on the plant but it will be several years before it blooms. In addition to spraying, foliar feed regularly through the year, so the plants can absorb the extra nutrients through their thick leaves and aerial roots.

As a plant extends upward along the vertical rhizome, the bottom part will become a bare stem, the lower leaves being shed naturally. In time there can be more stem than plant in leaf, at which stage the stem can be cut, separating the leafed part of the plant, together with a good supply of aerial roots, to repot on its own. If kept, the base of the plant may produce new growth, too. This is about the only time a *Vanda* needs repotting, otherwise it can remain in its basket and have the potting mix replaced without being removed from it. If the plant has outgrown its basket, place it and the plant directly into a larger one, filling in the space around it with the same chunky potting materials.

Vandas have a short resting period during the winter. It is noticeable when the green tips of the roots cease to grow and develop an outer covering of white velamen, which protects the exposed root and, being porous, absorbs moisture and nutrients. Insect pests seldom attack vandas when grown in humid conditions, but their roots are vulnerable to slug and snail damage.

From among a large number of closely related orchids which interbreed with vandas, ascocentrums are the most significant. Requiring similar growing conditions to vandas, they are similar in appearance but more compact and shorter growing. Their flowers are equally bright and, when crossed with vandas to produce ascocendas, the results are stunning, with many more flowers on a spike in greatly enhanced colorings. These jewels of the East are hard to resist but, with all the problems they can present to the grower, they remain one of the great challenges to orchid growers today.

Vanda Varavuth (left)

The beautiful Varavuth, raised in Thailand and grown wherever sufficient light can be given for it to bloom successfully, produces exquisite light blue flowers on upright flower spikes. Their color is similar to the delicate pigments of the blue Burmese species _Vanda coerulea_ from which so many of today's hybrids have been raised. In addition to the fabled blue, seldom found in any other orchid, the vandas may be almost any color or combination of colors that are unique to the genus. Varavuth is both warm- and cool-tolerant, growing well in both tropical and temperate climates.

Flower: 5cm (2in) wide
Flower spike: 15cm (6in) long
Plant: 30cm (12in) high

Vanda Memoria Lyle Swanson 'Justin Grannel' (below)

This superb hybrid typifies all that is outstanding about vandas, an impressive genus, in which can be found the richest colors of any orchid. The blooms are carried on upright flower spikes, their large size and rounded shape causing each bloom to overlap the next, creating a wonderfully dense sphere of bold, vibrant color. Through generations of breeding, the natural hues have been intensified and improved, along with the flower shape. The intense violet-purple shown here is made up of several layers of color, one on top of the other. It can be traced back to, among others, the species _V. tessellata,_ whose tessellated petals can be seen to have influenced this hybrid, raised in 1991 by Robert Fuchs in Florida.

Flower: 9cm (3¹/₂in) wide
Flower spike: 30cm (12in) long
Plant: 45cm (18in) high

Vanda Violeta 'Fuchs Sky' HCC/AOS (above)

The brilliantly colored flowers of this _Vanda_ have large round petals and sepals with a diminutive lip, an unusual feature among the more popular types of orchid. Their coloring is distinctly mottled, or tessellated, over the whole flower. The blooms open a slatey blue and take several days to mature and gain their true blue coloring. Raised in Britain in 1959 by David Sander's Orchids, this primary hybrid between _V. tessellata_ and _V. coerulea_ has been remade recently in the U.S., using superior nursery-bred clones of _V. coerulea_ and has become a building block for future generations. These orchids are high light lovers and grow best in tropical countries of the Far East, where they bloom freely, often several times a year, and where most of the hybridizing is done. In temperate climates they are less free-flowering and the lack of year-round sunshine restricts their growth, which makes vandas a challenging prospect for specialized growers. See page 181 for a close-up of this plant.

Flower: 9cm (3¹/₂in) wide
Flower spike: 10cm (4in) long
Plant: 45cm (18in) high

Vanda suavis (right)

This variable species was originally discovered in Java in 1846 by Thomas Lobb, one of the famous Lobb brothers, who was collecting for Veitch. Though grown less widely than the more colorful hybrids that are so plentiful today, it produces distinctively shaped and colored flowers, with a dozen or more on the stem. The species can vary in coloring from creamy white to yellow, with reddish or brown heavy spotting; the illustration shows a particularly well-colored form. The curiously shaped lip, an attractive part of the flower, may vary from blue-mauve to red-brown. *V. suavis* blooms during the fall and winter and is both long-lasting and fragrant. The plant, which carries its long semirigid leaves in pairs along an ever-extending rhizome, can become extremely tall but may be reduced by cutting the rhizome in half to produce two plants. This should be done only if each piece can be left with sufficient aerial roots to maintain a new plant.

Flower: 5cm (2in) wide
Flower spike: 30cm (12in) long
Plant: 100cm (40in) high
Pot size: 30cm (12in)

Trudelia cristata (above)

An attractive close relation of the vandas, this is a cool-growing, high-altitude species first introduced from Nepal in 1818. It was sent to the Royal Botanic Gardens at Kew, in Britain, and described in 1834 as *Vanda cristata,* but it was removed to its present genus in 1988 because of certain botanical differences.
It has long been appreciated for its ease of cultivation and willingness to bloom regularly and freely, during the summer and fall months. Its delightful little flowers with their clear green petals and sepals and the strangely formed lip, white with red streaks, make it popular in

mixed collections. The flowers are carried on short spikes that come from the axils between the leaves. The plant is compact, producing light green leaves in pairs; although a well-cultivated plant can grow quite tall, it seldom becomes top-heavy.

Flower: 2cm (1in) wide
Flower spike: 5cm (2in) long
Plant: 15cm (6in) high
Pot size: 8cm (3in)
Temperature: 10°C (50°F) min., 30°C (86°F) max.

Ascocenda Blue Boy 'Indigo' AM/AOS
(left)

Many hybrids within the _Vanda_ alliance exhibit the lovely blue color that is so welcome here, and so rare in other orchids. Only the vandas have provided the orchid world with the fantastic color range that extends from the palest sky blue to the vibrant color seen in this clone. The parents of the acclaimed American bigeneric hybrid, raised in 1967, are _Vanda coerulea_ and _Ascocenda_ Meda Arnold. Here the _Vanda_, which appears twice in its parentage, has become the dominant parent, the _Ascocenda_ having had little influence. Outside the tropical regions of the world, the warm-loving vandas can be sluggish to reach their full potential, or to bloom when required. Grown with such ease in places like Florida and Thailand, they represent a challenge in less sunny climes, but one that orchid lovers welcome.

Flower: 5cm (2in) wide
Flower spike: 30cm (12in) long
Plant: 45cm (18in) high

Ascocenda **Fuchs Yellow Snow** (above)

Adding a further color dimension to the already impressive range of hues found in the genus, this variety offers a speckled white and yellow combination, in which the dorsal sepal resembles the petals, and the lower sepals are tinged with yellow, overlaid with red-brown tessellating. This new hybrid was raised in Florida in 1991 from *Ascocenda* Phak Hai x *Vanda* Charlie Clark. The *Ascocenda* influence has been largely erased by breeding, leaving a large, *V. sanderiana*-type bloom, whose influence is clearly visible in the patterning on the lower sepals. The latter species (now called *Eulanthe sanderiana*) would almost certainly be in the breeding line of this lovely creation.

Flower: 6cm (2 1/2 in) wide
Flower spike: 30cm (12in) long
Plant: 45cm (18in) high

Ascocenda **Fuchs Flame** (below)

This is a further richly colored hybrid, raised in 1985 by crossing *Vanda* Laksi with the species *Ascocentrum curvifolium*. Since the parents of Laksi are *V. Thonglor* and *Ascocentrum curvifolium*, a double dose of this species has given closely packed blooms of dense, intense coloring on upright flower spikes. The hybrid is extremely free-flowering in good conditions; while mainly summer-blooming, it may also bloom at almost any other time of year. An important aspect of the cultivation of ascocendas is the humidity level, which should always balance the high temperatures that are a criterion for their successful growth.

Flower: 4cm (1 1/2 in) wide
Flower spike: 20cm (8in) long
Plant: 45cm (18in) high

Ascocenda Su-Fun Beauty 'Orange Bell' (below)

Allied to the vandas are several genera that will readily interbreed to produce further man-made intergeneric hybrids, which has greatly extended the variety to be found among this alliance. The genus *Ascocentrum* has a few especially brightly colored species that, when crossed with vandas, produce some of the most brilliant shades in the orchid family. Such a species is *Ascocentrum miniatum*, whose *Ascocenda* hybrids produce smaller but brighter flowers in fiery orange, red, and purple, preferred by many growers. Su-Fun Beauty, raised in Malaysia in 1984, comes from a long line of similar hybrids extending from *Ascocentrum miniatum* and *A. curvifolium* with, on the vanda side, *V. sanderianum* and *V. coerulea*.

Flower: 9cm (3¹/₂in) wide
Flower spike: 20cm (8in) long
Plant: 45cm (18in) high

Ascocenda Fuchs Sunkist 'Mike' AM/AOS (above)

This superb hybrid, raised in Florida in 1987 and awarded by the American Orchid Society, reflects the colors of the tropical sun under which it has been grown. Robert Fuchs is one of today's leading hybridizers in these orchids, his Florida nursery world-renowned. The parents of this hybrid are Yasathon and Laksi, and it can be traced back through several generations of *Ascocenda* before reaching any vandas. Best maintained in a warm greenhouse, this hybrid is but a sample of the gorgeous "jewels of the Orient" being produced for the home grower. Raised under shade cloth and suspended from overhead wires in open slatted baskets, these orchids adopt their natural epiphytic habits and, in response to regular soakings with water, produce long and fleshy aerial roots through which they breathe and absorb moisture. See page 183 for another view of this plant.

Flower: 9cm (3¹/₂in) wide
Flower spike: 20cm (8in) long
Plant: 45cm (18in) high

Christieara Renée Gerber 'Fuchs Confetti' HCC/AOS (above)
This trigeneric hybrid, raised in 1990 by Robert Fuchs, combines the qualities of *Aerides*, *Ascocentrum*, and *Vanda*. The colorful spotted flowers are waxy in texture, with a distinctive lip, inherited from *Aerides lawrenceana*, which has also given the plant its fragrance and modified the flower's overall shape. The flower spike, with numerous blooms, is held in an arching spray. The plant is more compact and may grow a little cooler than other hybrids in this group. See page 182 for another illustration.

Flower: 5cm (2in) wide
Flower spike: 30cm (12in) long
Plant: 45cm (18in) high

practic

The majority of orchids in cultivation are epiphytic plants used to an aerial lifestyle, and their roots have evolved accordingly. Even though the hybrids may be many times removed from the species through generations of breeding, they retain the same basic plant and root structure, which is what makes the cultivation of orchids different from that of most other plants.

Potting material

What constitutes a good potting mixture for epiphytic orchids has been debated since the plants were first cultivated over 200 years ago. And since experimentation with various substances is ongoing, orchid potting mixes are still being monitored and improved. Cultural practices also vary around the world, since materials available in one country may be unobtainable elsewhere.

The first requirement is that the potting mix should be open, well-aerated, and free-draining. It also needs to hold the plant steady in its pot and should retain enough moisture and nutrients for long-term absorption by the roots. It must also be slow to decompose, reasonably easy and pleasant to use, and readily available. The most widely used organic material that fits all these attributes is pine bark chips. This material is available throughout most of the orchid-growing world, generally in fine and coarse grades. It consists of bark chips from commercially raised and cropped pine trees which, in the U.S., is likely to be redwood cedar.

There are several variations on this bark-based potting material. A proportion of peat may be added, for example, increasing its moisture-holding qualities, which is an advantage for orchids with thick-rooting systems, such as *Cymbidium*

Shown right are several alternative potting materials. Bark chips come in three grades (center, left, and rear), while the man-made alternatives include horticultural foam, an inert mix of foam sponge and dried moss (front), and rockwool (far right).

Most orchids will do well potted in an organic material like bark chips (left), which is both free-draining and slow to decompose.

and *Zygopetalum*. It is also useful for busy growers who may not be able to tend to the watering of their plants so often, and need them to stay wet for longer periods. Other organic materials used as a substitue for peat in different parts of the world include beech husks, coir, and tree fern fiber.

A number of man-made materials make good, if unlikely, potting mixtures. These include materials such as rockwool, which is an artificially made fiber with all the qualities looked for in a good potting material, except that it is inert and cannot therefore contribute any nutrients to the plant. The advantages of this type of material are that the plant can be kept much wetter without any danger of infection or rot setting in and, as there is no slow decomposition, the compound does not alter over the years. The disadvantage is that the plants will need exactly the right amount of feed in a balanced combination to maintain a steady growth. It is best to use this type of potting mterial only after gaining experience using traditional organic bark.

Two types of rockwool are available, absorbent and water repellent. They can be mixed together or used separately, depending on the degree of moisture retention needed. A number of other inert materials are suitable for orchids, used either on their own or combined with a bark and peat mixture. These include both horticultural foam and expanded clay pellets, both of which are absorbent, help to retain moisture, and allow air to circulate around the plant's roots.

Any potting material should be soaked beforehand and used in a dampened state. Bone-dry potting mixture is difficult to work with and will take a long time to absorb water in the pot, which could harm the newly potted plant by retarding the growth of its new roots. When working with man-made materials, it can be harmful to inhale the dust particles, which is another reason to dampen them; for the same reason, you should wear disposable gloves when handling these materials. Mix only enough for your immediate needs because, if stored damp, the organic mixes will encourage the growth of molds that can change the acidity of the material.

When deciding which material is best for your orchids, follow the advice of the nursery that supplied them. Try to keep all your orchids in the same type of mix, but if after some time a particular plant is not doing well, consider changing to another material. But avoid constantly changing potting mixes in the hope of reviving an ailing plant, as the underlying cause of its ill health may lie elsewhere and continually disturbing its roots will only make matters worse. Never mix an organic compost with inert material when repotting. Do not, for example, fill around a rockwool-planted orchid with bark chips, because the two have different cultural requirements and are not compatible.

Watering

Orchids are slow-growing plants, many living for years following a regulated pattern of growing and resting cycles. While the plants are growing they need to be kept evenly moist at the roots, without the potting material becoming either too wet or too dry. The open nature of the potting mix should ensure that water drains through the pot within seconds, retaining just enough for the roots to absorb.

Watering probably causes more concern to the beginner than any other aspect of growing orchids because the unfamiliar pseudobulbs and unusual potting material do not make it clear whether you should water or not. While the more experienced grower may be able to tell at a glance whether a plant requires watering, it might not be so obvious to the beginner. The surface of the potting mix may look dry but can be quite wet underneath. Lifting the plant to test whether it feels light is a good way of deciding. If you are still unsure, weigh the plants on a kitchen scale! This will give you an initial idea of how often to water until you have gained sufficient experience.

Both overwatering and underwatering can cause problems. If too much water stays in the potting material over a period of time, an organic medium such as bark will decompose, causing the roots to die from lack of air. Orchid roots are valuable and, once lost, it can take some time for new ones to be made. Each pseudobulb develops its own roots at the start of the growing season and the plant will have to survive on these until the next new growths are active and can produce their own roots. Older pseudobulbs that have lost their roots are unlikely to make new ones in their lifetime and will simply shrivel. If your orchids

are in a modern inert material, like rock-wool, there is far less danger of the roots rotting; they can safely be kept in a perpetually wet state without the risk of overwatering.

Plants that have been underwatered over a long period will simply stop growing roots, and those in the pot will eventually dry up and die. Once the root system is prevented from taking up water for storage in the pseudobulbs, these will shrivel as reserves are used up. Shriveled pseudobulbs can therefore be the result of either underwatering or overwatering. A close look at the state of the potting mixture will

quickly determine the likely cause of the problem. While the underwatered plant will recover after a good soak, one that has been overwatered will need careful repotting and attention over a much longer period before it fully recovers.

The amount of water to give at one application varies according to the individual plant. One that has filled its pot with a solid rootball or has pushed itself out of the pot will be difficult to water because most of what is poured on will run off over the edge of the pot. If only a little penetrates the potting mix, it may appear wet on the top, but still be dry underneath.

Use a spouted can to water your orchids and flood the surface of the potting mix. The water will drain swiftly through, so repeat several times if the plant is dry.

The best way to water orchids is from the top, using a long-spouted can and pouring water over and all around the surface of the pot. With newly repotted orchids growing in a bark mixture, take care not to wash the bark pieces over the rim of the pot. It will do no harm to splash water onto the mature pseudobulbs, allowing the water to run down between them, but make sure you do not get water into the funnel of a growing pseudobulb, or the center leaf of a monopodial orchid, such as *Paphiopedilum*. Water lodging in any of these places can cause basal rot.

The easiest way to water orchids grown in the home is to take the plants into the kitchen, where you can water them on the draining board and return them to their growing area after surplus water has drained away. In this way you avoid the danger of orchids being left standing in a saucer of water, which prevents the base of the plant from drying out at the same time as the top half and could be detrimental to the roots. If the orchids are to be watered in situ, stand them on upturned saucers in a tray deep enough for surplus water not to spill onto the floor. Alternatively, you can install some way of draining excess water. This is more practical in a greenhouse, where the water can be collected and recycled if it is in short supply. This applies only to clean water: Never use artificial feed more than once—throw any residue on the flower beds outdoors.

The best time to water your orchids is while the temperature is rising. In the summer and on warm, sunny days, this can be at any time of day, but in winter, when the temperature may not rise very much at all, water only in the morning. By the time the temperature starts to drop in late afternoon or evening, all surplus water should have dried up. During the summer, much more water will be needed because the plants are actively growing and transpiring more, while some water will be lost to evaporation.

Try to check your plants almost daily. You will probably need to water about once or twice a week, depending on the state of the potting mix. In winter, some orchids will be resting, while others will simply be growing more slowly. Slow-growing orchids need to be kept just slightly moist, so water them occasionally. Those that are resting need just enough water to prevent the pseudobulbs from shriveling—or none at all.

Epiphytic orchids growing on bark rafts need to be sprayed once or twice a day through most of the year to keep them moist. In addition, you should dunk them in a bucket of water two or three times a week to ensure that they stay moist. When a plant is growing on bark and has a good aerial root system, it is almost impossible to overwater it, because there is nowhere for a quantity of water to remain. But it can be underwatered all too easily, in which case the pseudobulbs will start to shrivel and the aerial roots stop growing.

When you submerge a plant in water, be careful not to damage the growing tips of the roots, especially of vandas and other thick, semirigid rooting orchids. It may be easier to fill a large, shallow tray with water and lay the plant down with its bark and roots soaking, while the leaves remain above water. The roots of aerial orchids will adhere to their immediate surroundings, making it impossible to remove the plant from the bark without

This is especially true of the thick-rooting cymbidiums, which can become potbound after a couple of years, when underwatering becomes a risk. A newly potted plant, on the other hand, surrounded by fresh potting mix and with a less developed root system, can easily be overwatered if the same amount were to be poured onto it. Water a newly potted plant by flooding the surface several times until it retains enough water to soak right through to the bottom of the pot. The smaller the pot, the more often it will require watering. In a greenhouse, those plants standing closest to the ventilators or heater will dry out much more rapidly.

To water your orchids in situ, stand them on an upturned saucer, in a tray deep enough to contain any water draining through.

Fertilizing

In the wild, epiphytic orchids are deluged with water daily throughout their growing season. Drying winds and the sun that follows heavy rain ensure that they are soon dry again. With each downpour, water is washed down the bark of the trees bringing with it meager nutrients in the form of bird or animal droppings and decomposing leaf litter, which can settle around the roots and at the base of the orchids. In this way, the plants receive additional nourishment, but they remain essentially light feeders.

In cultivation, you must apply fertilizer according to the type of potting material. The traditional mixture using bark chips as a base gives a slowly decomposing material that releases a steady nutrient supply over a long period which, in itself, is sufficient for some orchids. Those growing in modern inorganic, man-made fibers are totally dependent on fertilizer administered to the pot for their nourishment. Both materials have their advantages, but with inert potting materials, you can be more certain of getting the fertilizing exactly right, whereas with the organic materials, you can never be sure how much a plant is benefitting from decomposition. It is an advantage to your orchids to fertilize them lightly, since more harm generally can be done through over-feeding, causing the roots to be burned by an oversupply of chemicals building up in the potting mix.

Balanced orchid fertilizer is available in liquid or granular form through specialty nurseries and garden centers. The liquid fertilizer comes in concentrated form and the recommended dosage often requires it to be diluted into quarts of water so that, if you only

breaking the roots. Where orchids have been established on a fixed tree branch, water them through a rose, heavily enough to penetrate the potting mix around the bark. Since this method is not remotely practical in the house, aerial growing is best confined to the greenhouse or sunroom.

Use water at room temperature for orchids growing indoors. If you collect rainwater in an outside container, keep a small supply indoors for immediate use. In some areas, where the ground water is hard, it may be an advantage to collect rainwater, but in urban areas, where the rainwater is contaminated with heavy

metals, it is safer to use water from the tap. Orchids prefer soft water and, if this is not available, you can convert hard water by placing a muslin bag, or a length of panty-hose, filled with peat in a water container. This can be left in permanently over a long period before it needs to be replaced. The water will turn slightly brown from the leaching of the peat, but this will not harm the orchids. Water used for creating humidity can be used straight from the tap, but you should avoid spraying the plants with hard, scaly water, which may leave a coating of lime scale over the leaves.

have a few plants, far too much has to be made up at a time. Do not be tempted to reuse the rest of this amount over a long period. Mix a new solution for each feeding and simply discard any remainder. In the same way, a bottle of liquid fertilizer should not be kept for more than one season, as its chemical composition may change slightly over a period of time. Granular fertilizer has the advantage that it can be made up in smaller quantities, which is easier for the small indoor collection, with none going to waste.

Orchid fertilizer can be nitrate- or phosphate-based. Nitrate-based fertilizers promote growth and should be applied to a plant at the start of its growing season, and continued until its growth is fully developed. Phosphate-based fertilizers encourage flowering in a plant that has completed its growing. Once the pseudobulb is forming and maturing, but before flower spikes are visible, discontinue the nitrate-based fertilizer and apply a phosphate-based one throughout the flowering season, following the rhythm of the seasons without being hurried; do not attempt to force a plant into flowering before its time.

Orchids need fertilizing only while they are growing and active. The start of the growing season may vary, depending upon the orchid. Begin fertilizing as soon as the new growth is seen to be active, with new roots at the base, and continue right through the summer months, gradually lessening during the fall; discontinue fertilizing completely by the onset of winter. Once the growing season is over and the plant is resting, or has slowed down its growth in response to the change of season, you should discontinue fertilizing for any deciduous orchids, such as *Lycaste* or *Calanthe*, and reduce it for *Cymbidium* and *Odontoglossum*.

The best way to fertilize is to water the solution into the pot, directly from the top. In some circumstances, it is more practical to spray the foliage and aerial roots where these are growing freely. Only healthy orchids should be fertilized—sick plants that have lost their roots have no means of taking up the extra nutrients and any feed will remain unused, eventually souring the potting mix and destroying any new roots that later appear.

Always fertilize when the potting mix is moist, before a pot dries out. Adding fertilizer to a dry pot can prevent it from dispersing properly, which again can damage the roots. Orchids that are otherwise healthy, but whose foliage has a yellowish color, may be suffering from a lack of nutrients. In this case, it can be beneficial to spray the foliage lightly with diluted fertilizer to restore it to a good healthy green. This is also a good way of nourishing a plant that has lost its roots but still has plenty of foliage.

There is no need to fertilize every time a plant is watered. To prevent the buildup of unwanted salts in the potting mix, give at least one good watering with clear water in between each application. This will flush the potting mix and ensure that all unwanted fertilizer is washed through.

Fertilizer is also available in the form of a slow-release tablet, placed on the surface of the potting material and allowed to decompose into the pot. This form is not ideal for orchids because it cannot be regulated, and you are not sure how much fertilizer is going into the pot or when it has stopped being effective. You have much more control with diluted fertilizers. Many specialty nurseries sell their own brand of fertilizer, which is ideal if you have acquired your plants from that nursery because they can continue to receive the same type of nutrients. It is in any case best to stick to one type of fertilizer rather than to be continually trying out different types.

Orchids that are resting and young seedlings that have been taken from the flask should not be given artificial fertilizer until they are growing well. This also applies to propagations, small divisions, and newly potted plants, all of which need to make their own roots before being able to take advantage of the extra nutrients.

The easiest way to fertilize your orchids is to measure an amount of granules into a measuring glass and add the correct volume of water, following the manufacturer's instructions exactly.

Spraying and humidity

Spraying orchids is no substitute for watering but an additional part of their care; it should become a daily routine. In the home, you can spray the plants with a hand-held bottle spray, wetting the foliage just enough to allow small droplets of water to remain on the leaves, but not so much that the surplus runs down them to create problems inside the new growths or the central leaves on *Phalaenopsis*. Lightly mist all parts of the plant, including underneath and around the base tray. During the summer this will help to cool the foliage as well as keep the leaves dust-free. Where orchids are grown in a greenhouse, spraying is even more important to aid respiration during hot weather. Spray at least once a day in the morning in summer, increasing this during spells of hot weather; during the winter months, restrict spraying to warm, sunny days.

Evergreen orchids, such as *Cymbidium*, *Odontoglossum*, and *Cattleya*, can be liberally sprayed for most of the year, while deciduous kinds, including *Calanthe*, *Lycaste*, and *Pleione*, should hardly be sprayed at all—their softer foliage will become spotted if water is allowed to lie on it for several hours at a time. A light misting on sunny days is sufficient. *Phalaenopsis* and *paphiopedilum* should be only lightly misted, so water does not run down the center of their growth.

In the greenhouse, spraying can be used to create a humid atmosphere. Drenching the floor and staging on a daily basis will maintain humidity and help to achieve an atmosphere consistent with good growing conditions. Use a hose with a wand attached

as a much greater quantity of water will be used. Since water cannot be liberally splashed around in the same way in the home, gentle misting can be applied more often to combat the drier atmosphere

Humidity

Humidity is synonymous with good orchid cultivation. It is not to be confused with spraying or watering, but helps to provide the right background atmosphere in which your orchids can grow. The surrounding humidity should always balance the temperature as far as possible. In the greenhouse, regular damping

Spray orchid leaves lightly with water on a regular basis to keep them fresh and free from dust (above).

Keep a humidity tray filled with pebbles covered by water (left) to create a moist microclimate.

down, which entails soaking the area where the orchids are growing, should be carried out more in summer and less in winter when temperatures are low and the light is poor. In summer, damp down in the morning, as the temperature is rising, repeating it on hot days at noon or early afternoon. As the temperature cools toward evening, the humidity will rise automatically, by which time the foliage and surface water should have already evaporated, and you may not need to put down more water until the following day. On rainy days there will be enough humidity without any damping down.

Indoors there is little humidity available, but this aspect of orchid growing becomes less important where the temperature fluctuates less. The more constant temperature within the home creates a different atmosphere and, provided plants are kept evenly moist at the roots while they are growing, they will not suffer from lack of humidity. Some orchids, such as *Phalaenopsis*, are less prone to fungal attacks when grown in the home. Where the orchids are standing on humidity trays filled with pebbles or expanded clay pellets and topped up with water, there will be sufficient moisture rising up to create a microclimate. Indoor growing cases can be fitted with humidity trays in the same way. Humidity becomes more important indoors in winter, when central heating dries the air faster, so spraying to maintain humidity can continue throughout most of the year.

The most difficult place to achieve a balance between humidity and temperature is in a sunroom, where the conditions are neither those of the greenhouse nor of the home. Light usually comes in from more than one direction, which increases the temperature fluctuation, but where the area is an extension of the house, it may well be carpeted and furnished, preventing greenhouse-style damping down. Orchids growing here are likely to suffer from dryness in the atmosphere and, if they are to remain in a sunroom for the summer, you should spray vigilantly and use humidity trays where possible.

Light and shade

Orchids need light but not full sun. Their leaves have adapted over millions of years to thrive in the dappled shade provided by the tree canopy of their natural home. In the wild, those orchids growing within the forest will have green foliage, while plants of the same species found at the edge of a clearing exposed to more direct sun will have leaves with a reddish or yellowish hue. These plants live at the extreme of their light tolerance.

In the home or greenhouse, aim to keep the foliage a good healthy green, avoiding any stress to the plants caused by too much light. In a greenhouse, the light comes in from all around and you will need to shade the glass during spring and summer, using a paint or cloth shading or a combination of both.

As a rough guide, it should be possible to glance at the sun through the shading without it hurting your eyes. The amount of shade should not reduce the light so much that the greenhouse becomes gloomy, and how much shade is put on will depend greatly upon its siting. There may be large trees outside which will provide much natural shade, in which case shade cloth should be sufficient to keep down the summer temperature.

In the home, light usually enters a room from one direction only, so there is little danger of the orchids becoming exposed to too much light, unless they are standing directly in the sun, close to a south-facing window. Here, shade can easily be provided by net drapes, slatted shades, or an outside sun shade. Provided the sun is not shining directly onto the foliage at noon in the summer, most orchids can benefit from the early morning or late afternoon and evening sun, when the rays will reach the leaves at an

angle low enough not to harm them. Some orchids, like *Cymbidium*, *Dendrobium*, and *Coelogyne*, can take more direct light than others. *Phalaenopsis* and *Paphiopedilum* require the most shade, and these should always be kept farther away from the window, or placed behind other plants that will afford them extra shade. Cattleyas are often thought of as tolerating high light levels, but they can suffer more than most from direct sun, which may quickly burn into their fleshy leaves.

In winter, in the greenhouse as well as in the home, give the orchids as much light as is available. During this time, most are resting, and it is the season for ripening the pseudo-bulbs and growths made the previous summer. The most dangerous time of the year is early spring because the sun is gaining in power daily, and the orchids, having not been exposed to bright sun all winter, can suffer from too much light coming in too quickly. It is good to put some shading in position before the danger of overexposure to the sun.

Orchids grown in the home can be given separate summer and winter quarters to take into account the light they receive. While a south- or west-facing aspect may be ideal in winter, this would give too much sun in summer. Either move the orchids to an east- or north-facing window for the summer, or leave them where they are if shading is provided. Here again, outside trees or hedging may provide partial shade. In the summer, place a

Keep your orchids out of direct sun by using some form of shading. Indoors, a venetian blind is ideal (right), while in a greenhouse, you can fit the glass with special shade mesh (left).

thermometer near to the glass where the orchids are to give an accurate temperature reading, which can be several degrees higher than it is a little farther into the room.

Orchids exposed to too much light or direct sun will show stress by their leaves turning yellowish or reddish, and if the sun burns a leaf this will appear as a black or brown area on the surface directly facing the sun. Those that have been kept too heavily shaded or in a poorly lit area of the home will look dramatically different from healthy orchids. Their foliage will be darker green, lacking luster or gloss. The leaves will be long and lank and the pseudobulbs will not have ripened sufficiently to produce a flower spike.

Temperature

For cultivation purposes, orchids are neatly divided into three main groups of temperature tolerance, depending on where the original species originate in the wild. Here the altitude at which the orchids are found is more important than their global position, and whether they grow high in the tree canopy, or near the base of the tree in leaf litter.

Wherever orchids are found naturally, even in tropical parts of the world, the temperature can drop considerably at night; this cooling down period helps the orchids to cope with several hours of higher daytime temperatures. There is also a temperature variation between summer and winter, and there are warm and cool days in each season, depending on the weather and the hours of sunshine. Therefore it is quite natural, indeed essential, for orchids to experience fluctuations of temperature from day to day. A comfortable temperature range between which orchids can be grown is from

One of the most important pieces of equipment you can have is a maximum/minimum thermometer. This will record the rise and fall in temperature when you are away, or at night.

10–30°C (50–86°F), a range that encompasses the various requirements of all the cultivated orchids, with the exception of *Pleione* and a few others that need a cooler, but still frost-free, winter home.

Orchids exposed to higher or lower temperatures than this over a prolonged period will show signs of stress, although the occasional hot day or cold night will not harm them. But if they are exposed to extremes of temperature over a long period, their performance will be affected and their growth will slow down until it ceases altogether. By the end of their growing season, a much smaller pseudobulb or growth will have been produced and premature leaf loss will occur. Orchids exposed to below recommended temperatures during the winter will take longer to produce new growths in spring and will also suffer from leaf loss. Cool-growing orchids that

are kept too warm in the summer will respond by not producing flowers, although their growth may appear to be normal.

The majority of orchids in cultivation are cool-growing, including *Cymbidium*, *Coelogyne, Odontoglossum*, and many more. Most cool-growing orchids require a minimum night temperature of 10°C (50°F) and a maximum summer temperature of 24°C (75°F). Intermediate orchids need a winter minimum temperature of 13°C (55°F), with a summer daytime maximum of 30°C (86°F), and the warm-growing orchids should have a minimum winter night temperature of 18°C (64°F), with a summer daytime maximum of 32°C (90°F). Where orchids from all three groups are growing in different areas of the home or greenhouse, the main difference in temperature will be at night in the winter. During the summer months, there will be little variation between their daytime temperatures, which are dependent upon natural conditions.

To maintain high enough temperatures in winter, artificial heating will generally be needed. In a greenhouse, this will be supplied by a heater; and for orchids, electric heating is the safest and most efficient. Avoid a naked-flame gas or kerosene heater because they give off fumes that can cause ethylene poisoning, resulting in leaf loss and bud drop. A sunroom can easily be heated by running an extra radiator from the central heating system in the house. Within the home, sufficient heating probably exists already. Do not keep cool-growing orchids too warm at night as this will affect their flower production, and the same problem will also occur if intermediate or warm-growing orchids are kept too cold. Orchids in the three groups should ideally be kept in separate areas, where their individual temperature requirements can be met.

Repotting and dividing

Adult orchids are generally repotted every two years in spring, at the start of their growing season. Repotting involves removing the plant from its pot and discarding all old potting mix, trimming the roots, and returning the plant to a larger pot with fresh potting material. Young seedlings and divisions need to be kept moving and are "shifted on" every six months in spring and early fall. Shifting on is when a young plant is taken from one pot and placed into a larger one without disturbing the rootball; it is used when the existing potting material does not need replacing.

A plant needs repotting when the potting material has deteriorated and is clogged with decomposing particles. If you can push a finger through the potting mix, this indicates that it has largely broken down, has no food value left, and is no longer aerated. Left in this material, a plant will quickly lose its roots as water does not drain through, and the material becomes sodden. Plants also need repotting when there is no room for further growth within the pot, or when the roots have become so cramped that the plant has pushed itself above the rim. Another reason is when a plant gets sick through incorrect watering and needs attention to its roots. Do not repot orchids that are flowering or resting, but wait until the new growth shows. When repotting an orchid that has outgrown its pot, consider dividing it to form several new plants, rather than simply increasing the pot size (see page 208).

The aim of every orchid grower is to keep the plants in harmony and balance. In the case of evergreen sympodial orchids, this is when there are several pseudo-bulbs in full leaf. As these age, they naturally shed their leaves, usually one or two in a season, until none are left, at which stage the pseudobulb is called a back bulb. Back bulbs retain food reserves and can be propagated to make new plants when an inactive eye at the base is encouraged to grow (see page 211). A plant should always have more pseudobulbs in leaf than out of leaf. If, over a period, several have lost their foliage, you should cut off all surplus back bulbs; otherwise they can restrict the new growth, and successive pseudo-bulbs will start to get smaller.

Deciduous sympodial orchids, such as *Lycaste* and *Anguloa*, are different because they shed all or most of their season's foliage at one time. While some do this at the start of winter when they enter their dormant state, others retain most of their leaves until spring, discarding them just before coming into new growth and flowering. These orchids can easily support up to four to six leafless pseudobulbs, but the plant size needs to be reduced once successive pseudobulbs start to become smaller rather than increasing, or remaining the same size.

Orchids that produce more than one new growth, or lead, will grow in different directions at once, and these plants can be divided (see page 208), provided that at least four pseudobulbs, mostly in leaf, can be left on each division: Never divide a plant into smaller pieces, or you will prevent it from flowering for at least another year. You can, of course, leave plants intact if you are growing them on

This *Cymbidium*, pushed out of its pot by its roots, is in obvious need of repotting.

into specimen size, provided there are more pseudobulbs with leaves to keep the balance. Pseudobulbs are attached by a strong rhizome which is usually below the surface and visible only in *Cattleya* and similar types of orchid.

Monopodial orchids do not extend outward to fill their pots, but are in need of repotting when the potting mix has deteriorated, or when they have been in the same pot for more than two years. Tall-growing vandas and similar orchids can become top-heavy, and by the time their pots are full of roots they need to be placed in a larger container. Shorter-growing monopodials, like *Phalaenopsis*, are mostly shifted on to avoid disturbing their roots. Where decomposed potting mix needs replacing, the plants are usually returned to the same size pot.

Repotting a cymbidium

Before you start, lay down a few sheets of newspaper to collect the old potting material and roots which are to be discarded. Have ready a supply of dampened potting mix, preferably wetted the previous day, a selection of larger-size pots and a supply of drainage material. This can be pieces of polystyrene used for packing or broken polystyrene tiles. You will also need a pair of scissors, pruning shears, or a sharp pruning knife; these tools should be sterilized, so have a cigarette lighter or a bottle of rubbing alcohol handy, and flame or clean the tool after each use. It is a good idea to wear disposable gloves if you are using a man-made fiber such as rockwool or horticultural

foam. If you plan to divide some plants at the same time as repotting, have a few spare labels and a waterproof pen handy.

1. Remove the orchid from its pot by holding it upside down and tapping the edge of the pot against the table. If the plant is not

Once the *Cymbidium* is out of its pot, a ball of tightly packed, healthy white roots is visible. Because no dead roots are visible, this plant can be shifted on into a larger pot as it is.

If you see any dead roots, cut them away using pruning shears, after teasing the roots apart. If there are many dead roots, the potting material will fall away as you work.

too rootbound, it will slide out easily; but where there is a thick ball of roots, simply run the pruning knife around the inside rim to loosen them.

2. Lay the plant on the newspaper and examine its roots. They should be white and firm to the touch, with active growing tips. Remove any that are blackened and hollow. The dead roots may be wet and soggy or, if they have been dead for a long time, they will have dried out, and the outer covering will pull away to reveal the inner wirelike core.

If all the roots look white and healthy, and the plant is not to be divided, you can simply slip it into a pot about 5cm (2in) larger.

3. First place a layer of pebbles at the bottom of the pot and, if room allows, add a little potting mix. Place the plant on top of this, with the oldest pseudobulbs against one side of the pot, allowing as much space as possible between the new growths and the rim; this is the direction in which it will continue to grow.

Use a pot large enough to allow for two years' future growth, but do not overpot. Place some pebbles at the base of the container for drainage, then put a little potting material on top.

Fill in with potting mix all round, pushing it in with your fingers by pressing down against the rim of the pot. Press bark chips firmly, but do not push rockwool-type potting mix down quite so hard.

4. Hold the plant firmly so that the base of the new growth is level with the top of the pot and pour potting mix all around the plant until it is steady in the pot. The pseudobulbs should sit comfortably on the surface, 2.5cm (1in) from the top of the pot, to allow for watering without washing potting material over the edge. If the plant is standing too high, it will not be firm enough; if potted too deep, the base of the new growth will be below the level of the potting material, which could lead to rotting.

Dividing a coelogyne

1. When repotting a larger plant that needs dividing, or its back bulbs reducing, remove it from the pot and decide where to divide it. Push the pseudobulbs apart with your fingers and thumb where you intend to make the split and, using a pruning knife, sever the rhizome in between the pseudobulbs. Continue to cut through the rootball until the two parts are separated.

Divide large plants like this *Coelogyne* by cutting through the rhizome that joins the pseudobulbs. Do not slice into the fleshy pseudobulbs.

2. Remove all old or decayed potting material from the main part of the plant. Then tease out the roots, trimming back all broken, cut, and dead ones with pruning shears or scissors to the base of the plant. Trim the live roots to a length of about 15cm (6in). Orchids do not make permanent roots and, although this

action may seem drastic, it stimulates the plant to make new roots, and allows more space in the pot for them to grow.

3. Having been reduced in size, the main portion of the plant may be returned to the same size pot, or possibly one slightly larger, making sure there is a 5cm (2in) gap for it to grow into. Hold the plant firmly and fill in with potting material. Because much of the rootball has been cut away, more potting mix will be needed to fill the space, and it must be firmed down to hold the plant steady. If the plant is loose in its pot at this stage, it will not produce new roots into the potting material.

4. Where a plant is divided into equal portions, repot the other divisions in exactly the same way, using a container of the appropriate size.

You can divide a large plant into several pieces, but each usable piece should be no smaller than four pseudobulbs.

Before repotting, trim back long, straggly roots and remove any dead ones.

Leafless back bulbs that have been removed will have no live roots, these having died naturally when the leaves were shed. If you wish to use back bulbs for propagating (see page 211), divide them up singly, reserving those which are plump and green. Trim back the dead roots, leaving just enough to anchor each bulb, and pot them into separate small pots, or round the edge of a community pot. The older, shriveled back bulbs will have insufficient reserves left to be expected to grow, so they can be discarded.

Repotting and dividing slipper orchids

Repot these orchids as for cymbidiums (see page 206). Divide large enough plants so that each division has at least four growths with a new, developing shoot visible. Remove back growths for propagating once the plant is out of its pot by severing them with a pruning knife.

Prior to dividing and repotting a *Cattleya*, cut the rhizome in the fall, while still in the pot. Repot in the spring, once a new growth appears on the back portion.

Repotting phalaenopsis

Orchids that have a number of aerial roots outside the pot can be repotted in the same way as cymbidiums, but without placing the aerial roots in the potting mix (see below). Having developed in the air, they would

suffocate and die if transferred to the container. Repot carefully so as not to break the aerial roots and leave them outside the pot. Give the plants a few days to allow damaged and bruised roots to heal, then water sparingly. Resume normal watering a week later. Spray the leaves often to reduce any moisture loss.

This upward-growing oncidium will attach itself to a supporting mossy pole by means of its aerial roots.

Repotting upward-creeping orchids

Many epiphytic orchids develop an upward-creeping habit, producing each pseudobulb slightly above the previous one. This can make repotting difficult where there is also an extensive mass of aerial roots. Here the older pseudobulbs may be buried deeper into the pot to bring the new growth level with the rim.

Alternatively, insert a mossy pole or length of palm fiber into the pot, onto which the plant can grow. It will attach itself by new roots in a short time and continue to grow upward with the extra support. If the plant becomes top-heavy, place a few weighty stones in the base of the pot to prevent it from toppling over.

Repotting vandas

Orchids like *Vanda*, which make thickened aerial roots, are best potted in slatted baskets to allow air around the base. Divide tall vandas horizontally when large enough to leave the top with plenty of aerial roots and the bottom with foliage and roots. Leave young growths until they have their own root system and at least six pairs of leaves. Stanhopeas also need to be potted in open baskets to provide an exit for their subterranean flower spikes.

Grow vandas in open containers—slatted wooden baskets or plastic aquatic pots.

Pleione pseudobulbs shed their leaves and remain dormant for the winter. Pot up when the dormant eye at the base turns green.

Resting

In their natural state, orchids cease growing during the dry season and hibernate in response to lack of moisture. After completing their season's growth during the summer rainy season, the mature pseudobulbs store enough reserves of water and nutrients to carry the plants through the forthcoming drought. In cultivation, orchids continue to follow this cycle of growing and resting, and it is important to allow them their dormant period. During this time they need little or no water, so give just enough to keep the pseudobulbs from shriveling. In winter they should be given as much light as possible to ripen the pseudobulbs.

The resting period may last a few short weeks or several months, depending on the genus. Evergreen orchids that have a brief resting period and retain their foliage from one year to another do not greatly alter their appearance, except that they are flowering during this time. These evergreen orchids include _Cymbidium_ and _Odontoglossum_, whose winter care is little changed.

Orchids that have a deciduous resting period are more easily recognized as their foliage is shed in the fall; allow the plants to dry out and remain dry until the new growth is seen in the spring. These orchids, which include _Lycaste_ and _Anguloa_, flower while they are active, and starting their new growths.

Many more orchids, such as _Coelogyne_, _Encyclia_, and _Cattleya_, have a long resting period but do not lose their foliage, although the occasional leaf may be shed at any time. Dendrobiums are deciduous, semideciduous, or evergreen, depending upon the type, and will remain dormant for several months during the winter. _Stanhopea_ is the exception, most often resting during the summer, and starting their new growths in early fall after flowering, to continue growing throughout the winter.

The very cool-growing _Pleione_ and the warmer deciduous _Calanthe_ are among those orchids that have the most complete rest. Their leaves are shed in the fall, and they remain completely inactive until the spring starts them into life. To allow total drying out, these orchids may be taken out of their pots and placed in seed trays in full light; they can be removed to a frost-free greenhouse or to a garage, provided there is enough light. Once the shortest day has passed, check them regularly for signs of growth, when they can be potted up for the growing season.

Paphiopedilums and related genera without pseudobulbs have no reserves of water and should therefore not be rested in the same way, but kept watered all through the year. They require less water in winter, however, as the plants take longer to dry out in response to the lower temperatures and light levels. The monopodial _Phalaenopsis_ do not rest for long enough to have water withheld; their cycle alternates between producing a new leaf and a flower spike. A short rest may occur between the leaf maturing and the flower spike appearing, but watering is maintained at the same rate, to keep the plants constantly moist.

Vanda and allied orchids rest from time to time, and this may be during the summer. The aerial roots become inactive as the green growing tip gets covered by white velamen. Lacking pseudobulbs, the plants still need to be kept moist and sprayed to prevent the leaves from dehydrating. When the roots send out green growing tips, the plant is growing again.

Because of the dry atmosphere, orchids resting indoors will need an occasional extra watering throughout the winter, whereas the same plants in the greenhouse will have the benefit of higher humidity. Light overhead spraying on sunny days also can be beneficial, but avoid spraying buds and flowers directly. As soon as you see new growth starting from the base of the previous pseudobulb, resume normal watering and fertilizing.

Vegetative propagation

Propagating orchids is a slow process, often taking several years for a new plant to flower, and is only worth considering with your best plants. Where growing space is limited, you would probably prefer to see it occupied by flowering orchids than by too many young divisions that will not give results for a long time. However, propagating can be a challenge for the orchid grower, and is well worth a try for favorite orchids that you wish to duplicate.

Sympodial orchids are propagated by removing the leafless back bulbs from the main plant at repotting time and potting them on their own (see page 208). Back bulbs that are to be propagated must not be too old or shriveled, but robust and plump, with one or more spare eyes at their base. These are the dormant growth buds held in reserve to be activated when needed. By removing the back bulb from the main plant and potting it in a moist potting material, you encourage it to grow. Cymbidiums are among the easiest orchids to grow from back bulbs and will take three to four years to flower. Most other types of orchid can also be propagated from back bulbs, although some grow more readily than others. Odontoglossums, for example, rarely succeed in the usual way.

Monopodial orchids are generally less easy to propagate, although *Phalaenopsis* and *Vanda* will occasionally produce a new plant naturally and can be encouraged to do so. Vandas may produce new growths from their base, particularly if the center has been damaged and is unable to grow. *Phalaenopsis*

occasionally produce "keikis," or young plants, from the ends of their flowering stems. Hybrids of *Phalaenopsis lueddemanniana* in particular will readily produce a number of these adventitious growths from one stem. While these methods of propagation are not as reliable as that for sympodial orchids, it is fun to try if you want to increase your stock.

Meristemming, or mericloning, is the mass cloning of orchids. It requires laboratory conditions and suitable skills of dissecting and culturing the small pieces of tissue removed from the main plant. Meristems can be bought as young plants to be grown on in the home, with the advantage that you are assured of the flower color. When buying young hybrid plants raised from seed, the color is unpredictable and all seedlings will be different.

Propagating from a back bulb

1. The dormant eye found at the base of a *Cymbidium* back bulb is protected by a brown, triangular bract which becomes visible once you know what to look for. (In *Cattleya*, the dormant eyes are green and particularly prominent.) Gently scrape away the outer covering to reveal greenish white tissue underneath before potting up the back bulb; if the tissue is black, the eye is dead and will not grow.

2. Once potted, place back bulbs in a small propagating frame and keep warm and moist. A soil-warming unit and moisture tray will further encourage new growth, which should appear within six weeks. When a new growth is several inches high, remove it from the propagator to a growing area. Repot at six-monthly intervals until a pseudobulb is formed, then grow on as an adult plant.

Note the greenish white dormant eye at the base of this *Cymbidium* back bulb (below left). Within 6 weeks of potting, it will have started into growth (below).

Propagating dendrobiums

1. Dendrobiums are sympodial orchids with elongated pseudobulbs, known as canes, and are propagated in a different way from most other orchids. Propagate the soft-caned *D. nobile* type and its hybrids in spring by removing an older, leafless cane, and cutting this into sections in between the nodes from where the leaves were shed.

Dip the severed ends into powdered horticultural sulfur to stop them from rotting.

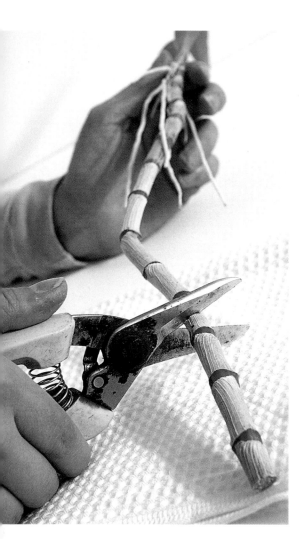

Cut a leafless *Dendrobium nobile* cane into suitable-sized pieces between nodes with a sharp knife or pruning shears.

2. Dust the cut pieces with sulfur powder at both ends to prevent rotting, and place upright around the edge of a community pot. Look for the slightly swollen nodes where sections are joined and bury each piece of cane up to a node, so when the new plant starts to grow it sits on the surface of the potting mix.
3. Alternatively, lay the stem lengths on their sides in a seedling tray. In a few months you will see young, healthy growth emerging from a node.

With the hard-caned *D. phalaenopsis* type of dendrobium, only the top portion of the older canes have dormant eyes. To propagate, remove this part and pot it. Dendrobiums often propagate themselves naturally, by producing growths from the older canes. But this can also occur at the expense of flowers and may indicate a cultural imbalance.

Propagating cattleyas

For best results, sever the rhizome during the fall, while the plant is resting, but without removing it from the pot (see page 209). By the following spring, the severed pseudobulb will have started a new growth which can be removed and potted separately from the main plant.

Propagating vandas

Where a plant has become very tall and has developed a length of bare stem at the base,

Bury the cut pieces up to a node, about halfway along their length, in a prepared container of potting material.

Within a year, this strong new *Dendrobium* will have its own leaves and roots to grow on to flowering.

encourage it to produce new growth by wrapping a piece of foam rubber around the stem, and tying it in place. Keep moist and remove from time to time to check whether new growth is showing. At this stage, remove the wrapping and spray regularly as a new plantlet forms. When this has produced its own roots as well as leaves, sever it and pot it separately.

Propagating phalaenopsis

To encourage a keiki (young plant) to develop from the end of a flowering stem, coat the nodes along the stem with keiki paste (obtained from specialty nurseries). In time a new plant, complete with its own roots, may start to grow. At this stage remove the new plantlet from its parent and pot it separately.

Producing and raising from seed

Should you wish to try your hand at raising a few orchids from seed, you need some knowledge of orchid genetics. You may not be aware, for example, that a *Cymbidium* will only cross with another *Cymbidium* and that this same-genus breeding is true for the majority of orchids, but that the *Odontoglossum* alliance contains many closely related plants, all of which will interbreed with each other to give bigeneric and multigeneric hybrids. The same is true of the *Cattleya* alliance, where there is a wide choice of crosses to be made. Further intergeneric hybrids appear among other specialist groups of orchids that are less widely grown.

Producing seed

If you are raising orchids from seed for the first time, it is easiest to start with a popular genus such as *Cymbidium*, whose seedlings will be relatively easy to grow (see the illustrations of pollinating on the following pages). Wait until you have two desirable plants in flower that you wish to combine to create your own hybrid. You may choose two of the same coloring to have a predominance of one shade, or combine two different shades for a greater variety.

However many plants you raise to flowering (which can take up to five or six years), each one will be distinctly different; no two orchid hybrids are ever alike. While they may share similar characteristics to their parents, each will nevertheless contain its own special

markings and lip, or petal decoration. It is this unknown element that makes orchid hybridizing so exciting, and every breeder hopes to create one outstanding plant that could become an award winner.

Pollinating the flowers of slipper orchids is slightly different because the pollinia are found on either side of the rostellum (equivalent to the column in other orchids) at the center of the flower, above the pouch. You therefore have to cut away the back of the pouch to place the pollen onto the stigma.

Raising orchids from seed

Raising orchids from seed is a skilled technique that requires a dedicated approach. After pollinating, keep a careful note of the parents and the date the cross was made. You now have a long wait of several months while the seed capsule slowly develops and ripens. Once you have a ripened seedpod, there is a choice of two methods of raising the seed. If you require very few seedlings, try the natural method (see below), where you need only sprinkle the seed straight from the capsule onto the surface potting material of the capsule-bearing plant, and in time a few seedlings may germinate and grow. This method is known to succeed best with the species, when vigorous seedlings can be produced. The artificial method of raising orchids from seed, practiced by commercial growers and leading amateurs, has a higher success rate (see page 214).

Raising seed naturally

Prepare the surface of the potting material first by covering it with a very fine layer of bark so the seed will find a good surface upon which to germinate. Sprinkle seed from the capsule onto the compost, then water by standing the

plant in a container and allowing water to soak up to the top; this prevents any seed being washed over the edge of the pot. Lightly mist the surface to keep it moist.

Raising seed commercially

In the artificial method of raising orchids, the seed is sown in clear sterile containers on a culture medium containing all the basic nutrients for the seedling's germination and growth. Specialty nurseries raise from seed in this way, then sell "hobby flasks" containing a small number of successfully raised seedlings. This is the easiest way for the amateur grower to acquire young plants to grow on. Each flask or wide-necked jar will contain 10–12 young plants, each about 2.5cm (1in) high and with their own roots, all ready to be potted.

Carefully remove the plants from the flask or jar by flushing them out with the jellylike growing medium and rinsing them in water to remove all the solution. Pot up the biggest plants on their own in individual 5cm (2in)

Pollinating cymbidiums

1. Select two plants in flower and choose the stronger of the two to carry the seed capsule, the other to provide the pollen. Using a small pointed stick, lift the pollen cap upward to remove the pollinia, which will adhere to the stick (above); place on one side.

2. Repeat this process with the other flower and transfer its pollen to the first flower, placing it on the underside of the column where it will stick to the small hollow, which is the stigmatic surface (right). You can pollinate more than one bloom on each plant to maximize your chances of success and, later, remove all but one developing seed capsule.

pots, and place the smaller plants round the edge of a community pot, using a fine bark potting mix suitable for seedlings. Place all the pots in a propagator and keep the young

plants moist; water carefully and spray lightly until new roots have formed at the base. The new roots will be more robust than those made in the growing medium and will be

recognizable as typical orchid roots, with white velamen and green growing tips.

The alternative is to send your own seed, from a plant you have pollinated, to a specialty nursery or an orchid laboratory that offers a seed-sowing service, for them to raise. There will be probably be a minimum order of at least five jars containing twenty plants each, making one hundred or more in total. This sounds like a lot but during the process of weaning from jars a percentage is always lost, so safety in numbers is the best insurance.

If germination is successful, after about nine months, the seedlings will be large enough to be removed from the flask and they will be sent to you to start their life in a more natural world. You will then take the seedlings from the jars or flasks and wash them out into a tray of water, before potting them as described for seedlings bought in a "hobby flask" on page 214.

As soon as the plants are strong enough and are growing well—probably after about six months—you can remove them from the propagator. The best time to move them to an outdoor area is in spring or early summer, when they have their growing season ahead of them. By the first fall, the plants should have grown steadily enough to be shifted on into a slightly larger pot and this should be done again the following spring, by which time their expanding root system will have more or less filled the pots.

The young plants should make their first pseudobulb within a year, followed by the next new growth. Each pseudobulb should show an increase in size until, after a few years, a flowering pseudobulb is produced. When you see the first flower spike appearing on your own hybrid, you can proudly claim to have raised your own seedling to flowering.

You may name the hybrid you have raised, provided the same cross has not previously been made, and, for a fee, register it with the Royal Horticultural Society in London, England, the world authority for the registration of orchid hybrids, with you as the raiser. This is surely the ultimate achievement in orchid growing.

A single seed capsule (left) may contain half a million seeds, which can be seen below in their various early stages of development. Sterile conditions are essential inside the jars.

Pests and diseases

Orchids growing within a clean indoor environment are unlikely to be bothered by many pests or diseases, but there are a few pests that seem to arrive from nowhere and, if left undetected, can build up into sizeable colonies that are difficult to eradicate. In most cases, there is little need to resort to using chemicals for controlling pests indoors.

A leaf affected by bacterial infection.

The most likely pests to be encountered are aphids. These sap-sucking insects can enter the house from open windows in spring and summer and will settle on buds and new growths, causing blemishes on young leaves and deformities on buds. They also excrete a sugary substance which can stick to the leaf and upon which a sooty mold will grow. Where just a few insects are seen, rinse them off in water, using a small paintbrush to dislodge any left behind.

Slugs and snails are a much greater menace in the greenhouse where the humid conditions are ideal for them to breed. They will attack buds and root tips, and larger ones will eat into the pseudobulbs, causing a gum-like substance to seep from the wound. Use horticultural sulfur to dry up the damaged part,

and trap the pest by placing slices of apple on the surface of the potting material. Slugs and small snails are attracted to this, and will have congregated underneath by the following morning. Other pests you may occasionally encounter include leaf-eating caterpillars and vine weevils. Look out for these and check the plants on a regular basis if damage is seen.

Pests that are harder to detect include red spider mite, scale insects, and mealybug. Red spider mite is a minute, reddish-colored mite that thrives on the undersides of leaves and prefers the drier conditions found in the home. Because it is so small you will usually notice the damage first. This is seen as a silvery white mottling on the leaves, caused where this sap-sucking pest has attacked the leaf. To control, wipe all the foliage with a paper tissue dipped in rubbing alcohol, then rinse with clean water. Do this weekly until the pest and its eggs have gone. The white mottling can turn black as a fungal infection spreads into the dead leaf cells.

Scale insects, up to 3mm (¹/₈ in) long, may be either hard or soft. The adults cover themselves with a swhite or brown shell and remain in one position on the leaf, moving on only after a yellow patch appears. They can be difficult to dislodge and may have to be gently scrubbed from the leaf with a toothbrush dipped in rubbing alcohol.

A leaf showing Cymbidium mosaic virus.

Mold on a Phalaenopsis flower, caused by damp conditions.

The young move freely around on the plant so it may take several efforts to eradicate scales.

Mealybug is similar in appearance and about the same size as scale insect. It covers its pinkish body with a white mealy substance and sucks the sap from the leaf, leaving yellow patches where it has been. Look for this pest in the inaccessible places between leaves and beneath bracts. Remove using a cotton ball dipped in rubbing alcohol.

Diseases in orchids are usually the result of neglect over a long period, subjecting the plants to stress, which makes them vulnerable. The most commonly seen is *Cymbidium* mosaic virus, which shows up on the new leaves as a white flecking that later turns black from fungal infection. There is no cure for this and any plant you suspect of being infected should be kept away from others until you are sure it is not infected, or it dies. The leaves of *Phalaenopsis* and the green pseudobulbs of *Odontoglossum*, *Lycaste*, and *Zygopetalum* may be affected by a disease that appears as a watery blemish and dries up to leave a brown depression. To prevent the infection from spreading, remove the affected area as far as possible and apply sulfur to it.

Keeping orchids healthy

A healthy plant should have good-sized plump pseudobulbs, increasing rather than decreasing in size, with the largest at the front, although it is acceptable for the oldest ones at the back to have shriveled through old age. The newest pseudobulbs are the most significant and these should be both firm and plump. Deciduous orchids, including *Lycaste*, should retain the plumpness in their pseudobulbs all year. If evergreen, like *Cymbidium*, most of the pseudobulbs should be carrying healthy leaves of a good green color and be neither limp nor dehydrated. Confirm an abundance of live roots by slipping the plant out of its pot to examine them without disturbing the potting material. Do not try this with a newly repotted plant because the potting mix will fall away and break up the rootball.

In *Phalaenopsis* and *Vanda* the leaves should be firm and a good medium green, with active roots showing around the pot or over the side. The foliage should not be pitted or dehydrated. With *Phalaenopsis*, there should never be less than three leaves at any time. The potting material must be firmly in place, supporting the upright plant.

A sickly plant will invariably be suffering from a stress-related condition. Yellowing or reddening of the foliage may indicate either too much light during the summer, or insufficient fertilizer being provided. The remedy is to place the plant in a shadier position and increase the fertilization until the leaves return to a good green. Premature leaf loss, where

Tie the flower spikes of odontoglossums, like this *Oncidium* Star Wars, securely to a stake for support, or they can snap under the weight of their blooms.

an evergreen orchid loses most or all of its foliage at one time, may be caused by overwatering, severe temperature fluctuations, or a combination of inappropriate conditions that the plant finds intolerable. To return such a orchid to good health can take years, so it is

often better to improve the growing conditions and replace the plant.

The shriveled pseudobulbs or leaves of *Cattleya*, *Phalaenopsis*, *Vanda* and others with fleshy foliage are likely to be showing dehydration, caused by over- or underwatering. An overwatered plant will have lost its roots through being kept too wet, and will need careful treatment to bring it back into good health. Repotting it into fresh material will encourage new roots to develop. The underwatered plant needs to have more water at its base. A good soak in a bucket of water for half an hour will plump up shriveled pseudobulbs within a week or so.

Black tips are often seen at the ends of leaves, and this is a sign that there is an imbalance of cultural factors. Trimming back the tips with a sterilized tool and finding a new position for the plant will often resolve the problem. Black patches on the leaf may be the result of sunburn, where the burn relates directly to the position of the sun on the leaf surface. The disfigurement will not turn green again, so remove that part of the leaf.

Orchids that are in a sickly state are not likely to flower, unless they are so weakened that they use their last reserves to produce blooms before they die. Here, the best advice

This *Phalaenopsis* has lost a leaf through crown rot, caused by overwatering.

is to enjoy the flowers while they last, then replace the plant. Healthy orchids will bloom in their season as a matter of course; those that appear to be healthy but do not flower are probably being prevented from doing so through being grown too soft, in conditions that are too warm overall or where the temperature does not drop sufficiently at night. Keep cool-growing orchids in a warmer night temperature than recommended or under too heavy shade can result in lush growth incapable of producing a flower spike. Lowering the nighttime temperature should encourage flowering the following season.

Phalaenopsis can benefit from a seasonal lowering of the night-time temperature by as much as 10°C (14°F) for two or three weeks at a time, which will almost always encourage a flower spike to appear. Most orchids, however, have a more defined flowering season and should not be encouraged to bloom at other times. Orchids that have missed flowering for a few years but have remained fit and healthy will produce an abundance of bloom as soon as conditions permit, giving you a great show all at once.

The flower spikes of *Odontoglossum*, *Cymbidium*, and others that produce a heavy crop of flowers can kink or snap under their own weight as the blooms develop, so tie these spikes to a bamboo cane for support. A small cotton batting wrap around the base will prevent slugs from reaching the buds.

Fungal infections can attack flowers, causing spotting and premature aging. This is usually the result of cold and wet conditions, unlikely in the home but common in a greenhouse where there may be insufficient warmth in the winter, combined with poor light. A drier atmosphere will help to prevent this problem. When a recently opened flower, expected to

Give an underwatered plant a good soak in a bucket of water, after which the pseudobulbs will soon plump up.

last for several weeks, dies prematurely, the problem will probably lie with the pollen. Pollens can easily be dislodged by accident when brushing against a flower, which then behaves as if it has been pollinated and collapses within days. This will also occur when the pollen has been infected with a mold, making it appear black rather than a healthy yellow color. The rotting of pollen is usually caused by a combination of cold and wet conditions, and occurs most often during the winter. These conditions are more likely to be encountered in the greenhouse, and the problem is rarely seen in the drier conditions of the home. Mice are known to take orchid pollen, which they find a nutritious source of food. Bees should also be kept away from orchids since they may pollinate the flowers, causing them to die.

Year-round orchid care

Spring

The most care will be needed at the start of spring when orchids become active, and there is more to do. Inspect your plants daily to ensure that they do not go unwatered and give their leaves a daily spray, or sponge to keep them fresh and dust-free.

Watch out for emerging flower spikes and mark their presence with a short bamboo cane to prevent them from breaking. Tall flower spikes will need supporting as they grow; always leave the flowering part of the long sprays free to arch naturally so as not to inter-fere with the natural position of the blooms.

As the flowers fade on the spike, remove them before they drop, and cut the old flower spikes down to the base. *Phalaenopsis* are the exception and, provided the plant is strong and growing well, it can sometimes support a secondary flower spike from a stem. To encourage this prolonged flowering, cut the finished flower spike back to a lower node and further blooms will develop.

Attention to detail now will ensure that any pests arriving on the orchids are swiftly dealt with and not allowed to make large colonies.

Repot those plants that need it as soon as they have finished flowering. Do not repot orchids with flower spikes unless they are in urgent need of a larger pot and can be simply dropped on without disturbing the roots.

Summer

Many orchids can be moved to an outdoor position in summer. Find a suitable place alongside a hedge or fence where they will receive early-morning or late-afternoon sun, and keep them shaded during the hottest part of the day. Orchids placed outdoors will need more frequent watering, and the fertilizer can be stepped up too, as the extra light available will create a harder and faster growth. Always ensure that the foliage remains a healthy medium green color. Check that small plants are not blown over by wind; if necessary, keep several little pots together in a tray, each supporting the other. Hose over the growing area daily to create a moist atmosphere from which the plants will benefit.

Orchids that are to stay in the house, including the soft-leaved *Lycaste*, *Anguloa*, and *Calanthe*, may be moved to a shadier position for the summer.

Summer care involves ensuring that the orchids are not subjected to too high temperatures. In hot regions, shade cloth will be required both outdoors as well as in a greenhouse. Orchids will cope with excessively high temperatures better if the humidity is also high to balance it. In the controlled environment of a greenhouse, this is more easily achieved; indoors, humidity trays and regular spraying of the foliage will keep the orchids cool.

Fall

As the fall approaches and the temperatures start to cool down, plants placed outdoors should be brought back into their indoor growing area.

If the orchids are to return to a greenhouse for the winter, and summer crops have been growing there in their absence, thoroughly clean out the area to make sure there are no pests, such as red spider mite, or fungal spores, which may be in the air. Wash down the glass and sides of the greenhouse with a household disinfectant to ensure the orchids can be returned safely.

Indoors, if the orchids stand on humidity trays, clean these out and rinse through the pebbles to remove any algae. Everything should be clean and ready for the orchids to return to their winter quarters well before the first night frosts.

At around this time, most orchids will shed a few leaves, or all of their foliage if they are deciduous. The change in conditions from outside to indoors will often trigger this foliage loss, and it is the plant's way of preparing itself for a period of reduced activity. If the leaves have turned yellow, either allow them to drop off naturally, or cut them off with a sterilized tool where the natural break occurs at the base of the leaf.

Winter

Winter care involves maintaining a balance between temperature and humidity. In the greenhouse, this means less damping down and no overhead spraying of the leaves. At this time of year, the water will remain for too long on the foliage before drying, which can cause damp spots on leaves and flowers.

Indoors, where conditions are drier, the change is less noticeable. Watering will be

lessened but daily light misting or sponging of the leaves can continue where the water dries up within a short time. Place the orchids in a light position for the winter; those that are resting will need just enough water to keep their pseudobulbs plump. Orchids such as *Paphiopedilum*, and others that do not produce pseudobulbs do not have a long rest and should be watered throughout.

When the weather turns cold, make sure that the orchids are not standing too close to a window, where cold from the glass could harm them. This should not be a problem wherever double glazing is installed, because the inside pane of glass will be warmer. Drawing the drapes at night will greatly assist in keeping cold away from orchids, provided the plants are on the room side of the drapes. To benefit from as much light as possible, open the drapes early in the morning and close only after all the light has faded in the evening.

In the greenhouse, water only on days when the temperature is a few degrees above the nighttime temperature, and do this when the temperature is rising, before noon. This will allow time for all surplus water to dry up before nightfall and will prevent the risk of spotting on the leaves.

Orchids that flower in this season will be of a better color and will last longer than those flowering in the heat of the summer, so you can expect the blooms to last for at least an extra week.

Once the shortest day has passed, watch out for signs of new growth. The gradually extending day length will encourage active growth, when the orchids will start to need more water and a light application of feed. Welcome them into the spring!

index

acknowledgments

The authors and publisher would like to thank Sara Rittershausen as well as all the staff at Burnham Nurseries for their help in producing this book. They are also indebted to Dolores Sanchez and to Jasmine Burgess for their help and involvement in photography. Grateful thanks are due to Jennifer Vine at the Lindley Library for the time she generously gave during research into the Royal Horticultural Society's archive material on orchids.

Photographic acknowledgments
page 34 Brian Rittershausen; 35 above Bruce Coleman/G Ziesler; 35 below NHPA/KA Callow; 36 right Oxford Scientific Films/Jim Clare; 36 left Oxford Scientific Films/Tom Leach.

Archive photographs
All archive photographs listed below © Lindley Library, Royal Horticultural Society: page 11 *Dendrobium infundibulum*, Orchid Album Vol. 10; 13 *Cattleya whitei*, Orchid Album Vol. 3; 24 *Cymbidium lowianum*, Orchid Album Vol. 10; *Cymbidium lowianum* var. *concolor*, Dictionnaire Iconographique des Orchidaées; 26 *Paphiopedilum* Harrisianum, Floral Magazine 1869; 27 *Calanthe* Veitchii, Curtis's Botanical Magazine Vol. 89; 29 *Odontioda* Vuylstekeae, Curtis's Botanical Magazine; 38 *Encyclia fragrans*, Curtis's Botanical Magazine Vol. 5; 39 *Cattleya labiata*, Botanical Register Vol. 22; 40 *Miltoniopsis roezlii*, Lindenniana Vol. 2; 41 *Vanda coerulea*, Orchid Album Vol. 6; 43 *Eulanthe* (formerly *Vanda*) *sanderiana*, Orchid Album Vol. 3; 45 *Odontoglossum crispum*, Horticulture Belge Vol. 14; 46 *Sophrocattlaelia* Thisbe, Nellie Roberts Collection, 1912.

Burnham Nurseries
A catalog and mail order service are available from Burnham Nurseries Ltd, Forches Cross, Newton Abbot, Devon TQ12 6PZ, England, telephone 0044 1626 352233, fax 0044 1626 362167. In addition to offering a wide and varied range of orchids in person or by mail order, the nursery sells a number of selected orchid collections, especially for beginners, as well as potting bark and other orchid-growing materials. Burnham Nurseries also offers a seed sowing and seed raising service for those interested in raising their own orchids from seedlings.